Homelessness

Editor: Danielle Lobban

Volume 398

independence
educational publishers

First published by Independence Educational Publishers

The Studio, High Green

Great Shelford

Cambridge CB22 5EG

England

© Independence 2022

Copyright

Photocopy licence

ISBN-13: 978 1 86168 857 6

Printed in Great Britain

Zenith Print Group

Contents

Introduction

Homelessness is Volume 398 in the **issues** series. The aim of the series is to offer current, diverse information about important issues in our world, from a UK perspective.

ABOUT HOMELESSNESS

In December 2019, UK homeless charity Shelter estimated that the number of people in England who were entirely homeless or in temporary accommodation was 280,000. A huge increase from the number estimated 10 years prior. This book explores different types of homelessness and the reasons people can end up in that situation. It also shares personal stories from those who have experienced homelessness and looks at the efforts being made to tackle this growing problem.

OUR SOURCES

Titles in the **issues** series are designed to function as educational resource books, providing a balanced overview of a specific subject.

The information in our books is comprised of facts, articles and opinions from many different sources, including:

♦ Newspaper reports and opinion pieces

♦ Website factsheets

♦ Magazine and journal articles

♦ Statistics and surveys

♦ Government reports

♦ Literature from special interest groups.

A NOTE ON CRITICAL EVALUATION

Because the information reprinted here is from a number of different sources, readers should bear in mind the origin of the text and whether the source is likely to have a particular bias when presenting information (or when conducting their research). It is hoped that, as you read about the many aspects of the issues explored in this book, you will critically evaluate the information presented.

It is important that you decide whether you are being presented with facts or opinions. Does the writer give a biased or unbiased report? If an opinion is being expressed, do you agree with the writer? Is there potential bias to the 'facts' or statistics behind an article?

ASSIGNMENTS

In the back of this book, you will find a selection of assignments designed to help you engage with the articles you have been reading and to explore your own opinions. Some tasks will take longer than others and there is a mixture of design, writing and research-based activities that you can complete alone or in a group.

FURTHER RESEARCH

At the end of each article we have listed its source and a website that you can visit if you would like to conduct your own research. Please remember to critically evaluate any sources that you consult and consider whether the information you are viewing is accurate and unbiased.

Useful Websites

www.awayhomescotland.org

www.bigissue.com

www.blog.scotland.shelter.org.uk

www.capx.co

www.crisis.org.uk

www.evolvehousing.org.uk

www.glassdoor.org.uk

www.gov.uk

www.homeless.org.uk

www.homelessnessimpact.org

www.housingjustice.org.uk

www.mentalhealthtoday.co.uk

www.mylondon.news

www.politics.co.uk

www.positive.news

www.shelter.org.uk

www.simononthestreets.co.uk

www.telegraph.co.uk

www.theconversation.com

www.theguardian.com

uk.depaulcharity.org

www.unherd.com

What is homelessness?

'It is a moral scandal that in 2020 so many people continue to sleep rough on the streets, and that is why I am determined to end the blight of rough sleeping by the end of this Parliament'.

– Robert Jenrick, Housing Secretary, 2020

Homeless is a term used to describe people who do not have permanent accommodation.

To be legally defined as homeless you must lack a secure place in which you are entitled to live or not reasonably be able to stay in.

'Hidden homelessness' describes those without a permanent home who instead stay with friends or family. Also known as 'sofa-surfing', individuals in this situation may not consider themselves homeless and may not seek support from services. Homelessness charity Crisis estimates that up to 62% of homeless people do not show up on official figures.

Rough sleeping is the most visible and dangerous form of homelessness. The longer someone experiences rough sleeping the more likely they are to face challenges around trauma and mental health.

What causes homelessness?

An individual can become homeless for a number of different reasons.

There are social causes of homelessness including a lack of affordable housing, poverty and unemployment, domestic abuse, poor mental health and mental illness. People can be forced into homelessness after leaving prison, care or the army – leaving, with no home to go to.

Many women are pushed into homelessness having escaped domestic violence or abusive relationships. Other life events such as mental or physical health problems or substance misuse can also put people under considerable strain and lead to homelessness. Being unable to afford rent, building up rent arrears, and having no other recourse is another common cause of homelessness.

Statutory duty

The Homelessness Reduction Act, passed in 2017, provided a legal duty that should enable all homeless people to receive help from their local council. This homelessness legislation specified that councils must try to prevent people becoming homeless in the first place. Councils started delivering their new duties on 3 April 2018.

In Scotland, there has been no distinction between 'priority' and 'non-priority' homeless people since 2012. According to homeless charity Crisis, this gives people in Scotland some of the strongest homelessness rights in the world. Anyone who is homeless can go to their council for help and they should be provided with temporary accommodation.

What can be done to tackle homelessness?

According to 'Homeless Link', the government should develop a cross-government strategy to prevent and end youth homelessness.

With regard to particular departments, Homeless Link recommends that the Ministry of Housing, Communities and Local Government provide local areas with long-term capital and revenue investment into a range of supported housing options.

It is argued that the Department of Work and Pensions could extend the Shared Accommodation Rate (SAR) exemption for homeless under-25s and care leavers announced in the Budget 2020. They could also match the Universal Credit allowance for under-25s to the amount over-25s receive, while maintaining the COVID-19 uplift of £20 per week.

It is further suggested that the Department of Health and Social Care could invest in greater mental health provision in non-health community settings, including schools, youth centres and young people's supported accommodation.

Lastly campaigners point to how the Department for Education could work with the Ministry of Housing, Communities and Local Government and the Department of Work and Pensions to ensure adequate preventative support is offered to children at risk of homelessness. Schools could also incorporate risk of homelessness into safeguarding procedures, as well as awareness-raising aimed at both staff and young people on homelessness and the support options available.

At the peak of the COVID-19 pandemic, the government's 'Everyone in Scheme' protected more than 37,000 rough sleepers. The UK government has spent around £700 million on homelessness and rough sleeping during the Covid-19 pandemic. According to campaigners, this shows how easy and practicable a solution to homelessness could be.

In his October 2021 budget, Chancellor Rishi Sunak announced the provision of £640 million a year of funding to address rough sleeping, homelessness, and the housing crisis.

How many people are homeless in the UK?

Estimates of homelessness vary, with the charity Shelter suggested that 280,000 people were homeless in England as of December 2019.

The Ministry of Housing, Communities and Local Government published the following figures in relation to statutory homeless in the period between July and September 2020:

◆ 68,680 households were initially assessed as homeless or threatened with homelessness and owed a statutory homelessness duty.

◆ 31,510 households were assessed as being threatened with homelessness, and therefore owed a prevention duty.

◆ 37,170 households were initially assessed as homeless and therefore owed a relief duty.

◆ 7,380 households had their main homelessness duty come to an end in July to September 2020.

◆ On 30 September 2020 the number of households in temporary accommodation was 93,490.

2020

Different types of homelessness

Many people think that 'homelessness' is simply another word for 'rough sleeping' (sleeping on the streets). However, sleeping rough actually accounts for just 7% of all homelessness in Wales. The different types of homelessness are outlined here.

Rough sleeping

The most visible and harmful type of homelessness, currently affecting approx. 2,900 people each year in Wales and representing just 7% of people who are currently affected by homelessness in Wales.

'Sleeping rough' means sleeping on the streets. This could be on the pavement or on a bench, in a bus shelter or even in a commercial waste bin. Sleeping rough often means being exposed to the elements and also to unwanted attention from the general public:

People sleeping on the street are almost 17 times more likely to have been victims of violence and 15 times more likely to have suffered verbal abuse in the past year compared to the general public.

According to new research from Crisis, drawing on a survey of 458 recent or current rough sleepers in England and Wales, almost 8 out of 10 have suffered some sort of violence, abuse or anti-social behaviour in the past year – often committed by a member of the public – while nearly 7 in 10 (66%) report that life on the street is getting worse.

The report shows that for current or recent rough sleepers:

◆ More than 1 in 3 have been deliberately hit or kicked or experienced some other form of violence whilst homeless (35%)

◆ More than 1 in 3 have had things thrown at them whilst homeless (34%)

◆ Almost 1 in 10 have been urinated on whilst homeless (9%)

◆ More than 1 in 20 have been the victim of a sexual assault whilst homeless (7%)

◆ Almost half have been intimidated or threatened with violence whilst homeless (48%)

◆ Almost 6 in 10 have had been verbally abused or harassed whilst homeless (59%)

Source: https://www.crisis.org.uk/about-us/latest-news/new-research-reveals-the-scale- of-violence-against-rough-sleepers/

In temporary/emergency accommodation

This can include night shelters, hostels, B&Bs, refuges (e.g. refuge for women) or accommodation from the private rented sector. How long an individual or household remains in temporary accommodation can vary significantly from a few weeks to a number of months and even years. There are currently approx. 2,300 households in temporary

accommodation in Wales (equating to some 10,000 individuals).

The negative impact of this type of homelessness should not be underestimated. Children growing up in B&Bs often develop long-term health conditions and face difficulties later in life. Homelessness can impact on educational attainment: accessing school places may be difficult; absenteeism from school is more likely; homelessness may 'single out' a child in a new school, increasing the likelihood of bullying and isolation.

Children affected by homelessness in this way are more likely to experience stress and anxiety, resulting in depression and behavioural issues, and more likely to experience homelessness again as an adult.

Hidden homelessness

The majority of people experiencing homelessness are affected by hidden homelessness. 'Hidden homelessness' can mean staying at a friend's house, sofa surfing, living in a squat or other unsuitable housing such as a car or shed. It may not be externally clear whether somebody is experiencing hidden homelessness, but this type of homelessness (as with all types) can be extremely harmful and leave a person very vulnerable.

The majority of people affected by this type of homelessness have also slept rough at some point.

In 2020 there were an estimated 3,250 households sofa-surfing on any given night.

At risk of homelessness

'At risk of homelessness' means that an individual or household is likely to experience homelessness if the appropriate support is not available/adequate measures put in place. Some estimates suggest that 1/3 of us are just one missed paycheck away from this, although it is difficult to provide an accurate estimation.

More than 30,000 households applied for homelessness assistance in Wales between April 2019 and March 2020 and, for this same period, the number of households who were given assistance due to being at risk of homelessness within 56 days = 9,993 households.

All types of homelessness can be extremely harmful and debilitating even if one does have a 'roof over their head'. It is imperative to acknowledge and understand the different types of homelessness in order to be able to respond appropriately and reduce suffering.

Dispelling common myths about homelessness

By Fiona Hobson

How much do you really know about homelessness? There's many common myths about homelessness out there. And those myths don't often portray homeless persons in a positive light. To add to this, most of these assumptions are all too often untrue.

We need to dispel these myths. They don't help us understand the true realities of homelessness or understand and empathise with homeless persons. Only by expanding our understanding of homelessness can we begin to support homeless people in a helpful way.

Why we need to dispel myths around homelessness

Myths about homelessness often simplify issues and promote certain stereotypes. We think we know all there is to know about homelessness, and these stereotypes can lead to prejudice and even hate. We need to raise awareness of realities of homelessness and dive deep into the complex truths. Myths are often wrong and can be harmful when they lead to a belief in negative stereotypes.

Dispelling the most common homeless myths

Homelessness is complex, and we'll begin to see this as we begin to dig into these myths. Here are some of the most common myths out there, and our insights into how true they really are.

You're only homeless if you sleep on the streets

The most common myth about homelessness is that all homeless people are rough sleepers. When most of us think of homelessness we imagine a person in a sleeping bag, bedded down on the streets. But, homelessness is far broader than this. This stereotype ignores a group referred to as the hidden homeless. The hidden homeless could be sleeping on friends sofas or floors, in rent-rooms or sex for rent situations, or staying in hostels and b&bs.

The myth that homeless people only sleep rough also distorts our understanding of the demographics of homeless persons. Rough sleepers are far more likely to be male, which means we tend to think more men than women are homeless. But homeless organisations believe more women are hidden homeless. We don't really know how many people are hidden and homeless. But, research by Crisis indicates that about 62% of single homeless people are hidden.

Giving people a place to stay is a simple solution to homelessness

Homelessness isn't simply solved by putting someone in accommodation. Placing someone in their own property is a huge change. That person is often housed away from the city centre. They're in areas away from their friends and community on the streets.

Added to this is the pressure of maintaining a property with little or no support. The transition from the streets to accommodation is difficult. Luke's story of moving into accommodation helps us understand the difficulties of living in your own place.

They're only homeless because they're lazy/don't work

It's hard to fully understand what it's like to be homeless. Imagine constantly struggling to find your next meal, shower and place to sleep. Then imagine keeping a job or looking for work on top of that. There's lots of barriers to employment for homeless persons. Lack of transport is a clear barrier, but so is maintaining clean clothing and a clean appearance for work. Often, people experiencing homelessness are vulnerable to exploitative working situations, as others capitalise on their desperation for work and cash.

Immigrants receive more support

That non-UK nationals receive a lot of support is a common myth. But, for migrants coming to the UK, there's little support available. The government's recent immigration rules make rough sleeping grounds for a non-UK national's leave to remain being cancelled or refused. There's limited support for migrants classed as having no recourse to public funds. They cannot access state support including housing support and benefits. This puts them in a very vulnerable position. We support many clients with no recourse to public funds who are destitute and have no clear path off the streets.

Common myths about homelessness fail to give us an accurate picture of the realities of being homeless. Homelessness is vast and it isn't simple to solve.

Experiencing homelessness is exhausting, making it extremely hard to hold down a job. And for immigrants with no recourse to public funds, there's little support available. Negative stereotypes about homelessness do little to help us understand and support those experiencing homelessness.

28 September 2021

Housing is a human right

'They treated me as if it was my fault for being homeless. They didn't treat me with any kind of respect. They treated me like scum to be honest.'

By Lisa Borthwick, Senior Policy Advocacy Officer at Shelter Scotland

Sarah's words, speaking to my colleagues at Shelter Scotland, show that the right to housing is often not realised for people on the sharp end of the housing emergency. Sarah was pregnant at the time, and she was still denied the right to a safe and affordable home.

Even though housing is a human right, specifically in the Universal Declaration of Human Rights, the law in Scotland does not recognise this right in the same way. Shelter Scotland still has work to do, to make sure that this right is fully realised, and to make sure that everyone has access to a safe, secure and affordable home.

But, earlier this month, Scotland came one step closer to recognising this right to a home, when plans for a new human rights bill were announced. Of course, this is still subject to the outcome of the Scottish parliament election, but the potential for this new Bill in strengthening the housing rights framework in Scotland is huge.

The proposed Bill will incorporate four United Nations Human Rights treaties into Scots Law, which include the right to housing as well as many other rights. It also includes further enhancing the rights of women, people with disabilities, and people of colour.

At Shelter Scotland, we support any Bill that strengthens the human right to housing in Scotland. In fact, in our 2019 'Are you with us?' campaign, this was the outcome we fought for. Many of you will have joined more than 10,000 people in signing our petition in 2019, demanding that the government make this law. We're so delighted that you have been listened to!

We know that one new law isn't the end of the story. But by putting all these rights, and especially the right to adequate housing, into law, there is further protection for people's individual rights and communities have a stronger foundation to defend their housing rights when the system doesn't work. It sends a clear message to everyone that we should all have a home which is safe, secure, and affordable.

This is the first step in a long journey – we don't know who will be in power post election, and the specific Bill has not yet been written. But there's much to be positive about: the National Taskforce on Human Rights Leadership has made many recommendations for what this Bill should look like, and the current government has fully accepted these recommendations. We've also recently seen that the message that housing is a human right is being used as a driver for Scotland's new long-term housing strategy – 'housing to 2040'.

There is plenty of work to be done to ensure that any new law helps to combat the housing injustices we see every day and to ensure that this new law makes its way through parliament. But for now, it shows that when we work together, we can truly make progress.

23 April 2021

Homelessness facts and statistics: the numbers you need to know

Experts worry about a looming crisis of homelessness. These are the rough-sleeping figures and homelessness facts you need to know.

By Liam Geraghty

Despite living in the world's sixth biggest economy, people are still living with no place to call their home in this country. This injustice must end.

But before you can tackle a problem, you must first learn the scale of the issue. That's why it is vital that we know the facts and figures about homelessness.

The Big Issue is committed to tackling poverty and preventing homelessness. With the prospect of rising homelessness in autumn 2021, The Big Issue has launched the Stop Mass Homelessness campaign. Thousands of people who have been affected by the Covid-19 pandemic risk losing their home after support introduced during the pandemic such as the £20 universal credit increase and the furlough scheme was withdrawn. The Big Issue is battling to help them keep their home.

Here are the numbers you need to know:

How many people are homeless?

♦ In terms of street homelessness, official rough-sleeping statistics showed the number of people living on the streets fell in England during the Covid-19 pandemic with an estimated 2,688 people sleeping rough on a single night in autumn 2020. This was a 37 per cent decrease on the 4,266 people recorded in 2019 and was the third straight year in which the count showed a decrease.

♦ However, the 2020 figure was still 52 per cent higher than the 1,247 people counted as sleeping rough in 2010. Rough sleeping has increased steadily over the last decade.

♦ The majority of people sleeping rough in England are male, aged over 26 years old and from the UK. Meanwhile the Office for National Statistics found men who are living on the street outnumber women at a ratio of six to one.

♦ However, the official figures are thought to be an underestimate as they are based on single-night snapshot accounts and estimates. Lucy Abraham, chief executive of London homelessness charity Glass Door, told The Big Issue in response to the 2020 figures: 'We need to be critical of using what is essentially a best guess of what rough sleeping looks like on a given night as a proxy for how many people are actually homeless in the UK. '

♦ The London-only Combined Homelessness and Information Network (CHAIN) figures are considered to be more accurate. They showed 11,018 people were seen sleeping rough in London between April 2020 and March 2021, an increase on the 10,726 people spotted by outreach workers and charities in the previous year. The figures show rough sleeping has increased by 94 per cent in the last decade – almost double the number of people living on the streets in the English capital 10 years ago. In Wales, the official count has been suspended due to the Covid-19 pandemic but recent management statistics show that around 128 people are sleeping rough around the country as of September 2021.

♦ And while Scotland doesn't use the same method as England and Wales, data from the Scottish Household Survey suggests just over 700 people bedding down on the streets in a single night. Amounting to around 5,300 adults sleeping rough at least once per year.

♦ As for wider homelessness, English councils helped 268,560 households to prevent or relieve homelessness between April 2020 and March 2021.

♦ In Wales, 13,161 households were assessed as homeless and were owed council support to help them into secure accommodation in 2020/21.

♦ As for Scotland, there has been a fall in the number of people applying to local authorities for support with homelessness but a rise in people living in temporary accommodation during the pandemic. The 33,792 homelessness applications to councils recorded between April 2020 and March 2021 represented an almost 10 per cent decrease on 2019/20 statistics.

Spending on homelessness

♦ Local authority expenditure on homelessness-related services has reduced significantly as compared to expenditure ten years ago; in 2008/9, £2.9 billion (in current prices) was spent on homelessness-related activity, while in 2018/19, £0.7 billion less was spent (Homeless Link).

♦ In 2018/19, nearly £1 billion less was spent on support services for single homeless people than was spent in 2008/09 (Homeless Link).

♦ The UK government has spent around £700 million on homelessness and rough sleeping during the Covid-19 pandemic and plans to spend a further £750 million in 2021. For the next three years, funding will be £640 million annually.

♦ Westminster ministers have also promised to spend £316 million in preventing homelessness in 2022/23 with money distributed to councils to help people find a new home or secure temporary accommodation as well as supporting people facing eviction.

Homelessness and Covid-19

♦ The UK government's Everyone In scheme has protected more than 37,000 people during the pandemic. As of January 2021, 11,263 people remained in emergency accommodation and 26,167 people had been moved on to permanent accommodation through the scheme.

♦ The government has promised 3,300 long-term homes will be made available to help rough sleepers protected from the virus.

- In Scotland, £50m has been spent by the Scottish Government on hardship funding and £22m on the Scottish Welfare Fund to tackle homelessness during the Covid-19 pandemic. Additionally, more than £875,000 has been spent providing support for people who are living with no recourse to public funds and cannot claim benefits. The Welsh Government initially spent £10m on providing accommodation to over 800 people at the start of the Covid-19 pandemic. This was followed up with £20m to ensure that people did not have to return to the streets once the pandemic has ended.

- A move away from temporary accommodation is being funded by a £50m investment as part of Phase 2 of Wales' homelessness action plan.

Homelessness and health

- Three quarters of homeless people quizzed in a 2014 Homeless Link survey reported a physical health problem

- Meanwhile, 80 per cent of respondents reported some form of mental health issue, while 45 per cent had been officially diagnosed with a condition

- 39 per cent said they take drugs or are recovering from a drug problem, while 27 per cent have or are recovering from an alcohol problem.

- 35 per cent had been to A&E and 26 per cent had been admitted to hospital in the six months before they took part in the survey

What do people think about homelessness?

A poll from Ipsos Mori and the Centre for Homelessness Impact, published in April 2021, set out to understand the British public's perception of homelessness.

The research found just under nine in ten people agreed homelessness is a serious problem in the UK and almost three quarters said they believe it does not get the attention it deserves.

The British public also believe homelessness is a consequence of societal issues outside a person's control rather than down to a person's poor choices, with 52 per cent blaming wider problems in the poll compared to 17 per cent on the individual.

More than half (56 per cent) saw homelessness as affecting the whole of society, compared to 20 per cent believing it only impacts on the person experiencing it.

The public also supported investing money in preventing homelessness rather than paying to deal with the issue when it reaches crisis stage with 61 per cent in favour of that approach.

The study is part of the Centre for Homelessness Impact's End It with Evidence campaign with polling company Ipsos Mori, aiming to use data to bring about a sustainable end to homelessness.

What is hidden homelessness?

Hidden homelessness is the term used to describe people who do not have a permanent home and instead stay with friends or family.

Also known as sofa surfing, many people in this situation may not consider themselves homeless and may not seek support from services. This makes it difficult to know exactly how many people are homeless, especially as they are not on the streets like rough sleepers and, therefore, not visible to frontline homelessness outreach workers.

Homelessness charity Crisis has estimated that as many as 62 per cent of single homeless people do not show up on official figures and run the risk of slipping through the cracks.

How do most people who are homeless die?

Nearly one in three people die from treatable conditions, according to a 2019 University College London study. Researchers warned that more preventative work was needed to protect physical health and long-term condition management, especially for more common conditions such as cardiovascular disease.

Homeless deaths have only been counted in recent years. The Bureau of Investigative Journalism's pioneering Dying Homeless project counted the deaths of 796 people in 18 months before handing over the project to the Museum of Homelessness in March 2019.

MOH's latest count revealed 976 people died across England, Wales, Scotland and Northern Ireland in 2020 – a rise of 37 per cent on the previous 2019 tally.

The count showed only three per cent of deaths were related to the Covid-19 virus with suicide accounting for 15 per cent of deaths and drug and alcohol abuse contributing to 36 per cent of cases where a cause of death was confirmed.

MOH used a combination of freedom of information requests, local news reports and submissions from the public to produce a count covering all kinds of homelessness, ranging from rough sleeping to people living in hostels and temporary accommodation. That method differs from the official counts where death certificates are analysed for signs a person died without a stable home.

The first official Office for National Statistics figures for England and Wales arrived three months before the end of TBIJ's project, reporting 597 estimated deaths in 2017. The most recent count reported 688 people died without a secure home in 2020 with Covid accounting for just 13 deaths.

The first-ever official homeless deaths count in Scotland arrived in 2020 using a similar methodology to the Office for National Statistics.

The latest count reported an almost 20 per cent increase in deaths with an estimated 256 people dying without a stable home in 2020. Despite the pandemic, no deaths were attributed to Covid-19 with drug-related deaths dominating the figures.

24 December 2021

The Tories' shameful record on the homeless

Will Covid will make us realise that something must be done about the poor?

By James Bloodsworth

Almost four years ago, I spent several dank hours sitting on a grubby slab of pavement in the summer rain of Blackpool listening to a homeless man recounting his journey from respectable affluence to gut-wrenching poverty. His name was Gary. Every night he bedded down in one of several foul-smelling doorways just off Blackpool's famous Golden Mile. As if to complete the gloomy mise en scène, he shared this particular doorway with a weather-beaten man whose frame filled his clothes like twigs in a sack.

What struck me was not so much the squalor of his situation: we're all familiar with the pornography of street life – the dirt and the poverty. What was extraordinary, though, was the suddenness with which Gary had fallen through society's floorboards. One minute he had a reasonably decent job, a relationship and a flat; the next, everything had unravelled like a poorly knitted scarf. By the time I met Gary he was eking out his existence in a rank doorway, unseen by the thousands who trod the pavements each day.

Yet Gary's experience was not an unusual one. Before Covid, the situation for working renters in Britain was precarious: almost half of them were just a single pay cheque away from homelessness. If you were lucky, you could 'couch surf' at the house of friends and relatives or, if you weren't on friendly terms with any good samaritans, then the streets beckoned. As wages stagnated, and the cost of renting increased, so too did the numbers of men and women bedding down in shop and restaurant doorways; rough sleeping in England rose for seven consecutive years up to 2017.

The most up to date figures show that from April to June 2019, 68,170 households were either homeless or threatened with homelessness – an increase of 11% on the previous year. This doesn't take account of the so-called hidden homeless: those couch surfers, squatters and those who bed down each night in filthy and overcrowded doss houses.

Homelessness now blights every large British town or city – and the public have tolerated it by and large. Or, at least, they have turned out to polling stations to vote for politicians who have tolerated it: David Cameron and George Osborne, for example. But their version of modern, caring conservatism seemed to view poverty through a decidedly Victorian lens. Responsibility was placed on the individual – 'and having located the responsibility, society goes contentedly on about its own affairs ', as Jack London wrote in *The People of the Abyss*, his journalistic sojourn among the homeless in turn-of-the-century London. And since 2016, all politicians of all stripes have been preoccupied almost entirely with Brexit.

But crises are funny things. As Covid-19 reached Britain, it started to dawn on politicians that the homeless were no longer a mere inconvenience to be edged past on the rush to the office, but potential super-spreaders of a highly infectious disease. So, on March 26, the Government issued its 'Everybody In' directive. Local authorities were instructed to provide immediate accommodation for anyone who was sleeping rough. Councils were handed a total of £3.2m to place them in hotels and B&Bs. Homelessness was abolished at the stroke of a pen.

To be fair to Boris Johnson, he had just announced new money to tackle homelessness before Covid arrived. In a break with its austere predecessors, the Government, in December, set up a £63 million grant scheme to help the homeless in England into accommodation.

However, as we ease out of lockdown, the Government is no longer directing councils to accommodate the homeless beyond their statutory duty. And the problem will spike massively as the pandemic abates. Crisis chief executive Jon Sparkes told me: 'At this very minute tens of thousands of people across Great Britain are struggling against a rising tide of job insecurity and high rents, all of which threaten to push them into homelessness.'

Against this ominous backdrop, though, there is much talk about the nature of the post-pandemic landscape. And a quiet revolution seems to be taking place. The number of people who see Britain as a society in which we look after each other has tripled since February. Since the referendum, conventional wisdom had it that Britain was a deeply polarised place. Yet more than half (57%) of Britons now believe the country will be united once the pandemic has receded.

We may, in other words, be undergoing what former prime minister James Callaghan called a 'sea change ' in attitudes: 'a shift in what the public wants and what it approves of '. Perhaps the sight of ragged men and women wandering submissively through British streets, paper cups gripped tightly in emaciated outstretched hands, may be intolerable to the nation that emerges from lockdown: a nation which feels itself both more united and more uneasy about the spread of disease.

But putting a roof over someone's head is in some ways the easy part. And in any case, the the idea we might ever totally eliminate homelessness is a pipe dream. Many are sleeping rough because of debilitating drug addictions. Nearly a third (32%) of all deaths among homeless people in England in 2017 were a result of drug poisoning. And many are there because of mental health issues or complicated social factors.

Turning someone who has existed on the margins into a functioning member of society – capable of holding down a job and paying the rent on time – is a bigger challenge. As the founder of the Big Issue John Bird wrote in 2017: 'The people I have spoken with or noticed recently know what they want. They want a further high. But that is the worst thing for them. Their decision-making has been robbed from them. Cogent and rational behaviour has been stolen away. '

But ensuring that every person in Britain has a roof over their head is something to shoot for at least. Money, too, is infinitely more useful than moral sanctimony when it comes to rehabilitating drug users.

The record of the previous Labour government is impressive in this respect. It also presents a historical refutation to the idea that blame for homelessness can be laid at the feet of the individual. Homelessness rose exponentially in the 1980s and early 1990s, resulting in the infamous 'cardboard cities' scattered around London. Unemployment played a big role, as did the increased availability of drugs. But the political will to reduce the problem just wasn't there.

In contrast, when Labour came to office in 1997 there was a conscious drive to end rough sleeping. They didn't quite achieve that – I'm doubtful that any government ever has – but there was a reduction by two-thirds in rough sleeping between 1999 and 2002, taking 1,147 people off the streets. This looks all the more impressive when set against the lethargy of recent years. The number of rough sleepers has gradually risen from 1,768 in 2010, when Labour left office, to 4,677 in 2018.

Today, there are a range of new factors driving people onto the streets. The 'gig' economy, for example, has become synonymous with chronic underemployment, while waves of migration from Eastern Europe have resulted in begging as newcomers discover that British streets are not paved with gold. Moreover, government cuts to local authority budgets, the introduction of Universal Credit along with house price inflation sent many more fanning out into the streets.

There are signs the public is growing tired of it – fed up of the sight of filthy mattresses and sleeping bags nestled under every underpass and alcove. Some of the shift in attitudes towards the homeless at the turn of the 1990s was motivated by an outburst of warmth for fellow man – the view that people were poor because they were simply unlucky gained public traction following the recessions of the time.

But many just wanted the streets tidied up. They were sick of seeing the destitute sprawled across the pavement each time they walked along a busy street or opened up a shop or restaurant. With contagion likely to be an ongoing existential concern once the pandemic has loosened its grip, it's hard to see how the status quo of recent years – the uncaring attitude that dismisses the street-dweller with a contemptuous wave of the hand – can continue in perpetuity.

Some have compared the coronavirus crisis with the Second World War. The Queen even nodded to Vera Lynn during her April 5 Coronavirus broadcast. These parallels can be pretty overcooked. For one thing, it's extremely unlikely that Boris Johnson will be viewed by history as a stoic Churchillian bulldog who pulled the nation back from the brink of catastrophe – although our unpreparedness to deal with Covid-19 does bring to mind the title of Churchill's book on the complacency that led up to war: 'While England Slept'.

However, I think key echoes may actually be found in Covid-19's aftermath. Britain discovered during World War Two that economic planning could work. And so, once Britain had seen off Hitler and the Nazis, it was no longer inconceivable that the Government could take a larger role in the economy. The old world of laissez faire economics was buried under ten square miles of rubble along with Berlin.

As unemployment soars, the political horizons of the British people may very well expand. Recent months have demonstrated to even the most sceptical, that it is possible to house rough sleepers. What it requires is political will – and for the Chancellor to turn the funding taps on. The homeless charity Crisis has estimated that it would cost £282m to permanently rehouse those currently staying in hotels and B&Bs. This is chicken feed in the context of the vast sums that have already been spent.

The next decade is going to be an exceedingly difficult one. Unemployment will reach levels not seen since the 1980s. The warm bubble we are suspended in at present – held afloat by furlough money – will pop come October, and many will fall suddenly to the ground with a painful crash. Amid the growing government debt, we can expect a rehash of the pro-austerity arguments of a decade ago; there will be calls for the Government to retreat yet further from the social life of the nation.

But I suspect the post-Covid landscape will resemble the post-war era more than the world born of the 2008 recession, at least in terms of its political potential. The greatest feats of the immediate post-war government – the NHS, the welfare state, a major programme of house building – were achieved in a country that was so bankrupt it had to ration bread. Yet within a few years, those radical institutions seemed entirely normal. The political horizons of ordinary people had slowly expanded as the bombs fell on British cities, to the point where an impossible dream – of a land 'fit for heroes', as Lloyd George defined it at the close of the First World War – had become a reality.

Perhaps Covid-19 will lead to a similar expansion in the realm of the possible. Amid the ever-present threat of disease, the comfortably off may begin to notice – really notice – the people who sit mournfully in the shop doorways. The sight of thousands of men and women bedding down out of doors each night might suddenly seem intolerable in a modern and civilised country. We may collectively look upon the Garys – as well as the thousands of other men and women like him – and put aside the miserly economic calculations and simply say, 'That is a human being '.

And then, just as they did for a few years after 1945, the poor will have begun to make history again.

23 June 2020

What the latest statistics tell us about homelessness trends in Wales

The Centre for Homelessness Impact

The Welsh Government recently released official statistics on statutory homelessness provision between April 2019 and March 2020 in Wales.

As these statistics are largely pre-pandemic figures, it is fair to assume that the picture may now look different than it did at the end of the reporting year (31 March 2020). We have already noted changes in other areas of the UK where more recent data is available. We are seeing more people in temporary accommodation in England and Northern Ireland, more people with low support needs experiencing street homelessness in London. As the pandemic continues to affect people as well as service delivery, local authorities are likely to continue facing mounting homelessness challenges in the coming months.

The figures released from the Welsh Government show that 31,320 households applied for homelessness assistance in Wales between April 2019 and March 2020. These numbers are stable when compared to 31,170 households in the previous year (April 2018 - March 2019). Over the same period, applications were also stable in Scotland while England observed an increase of +4% of homelessness applications.

However, this overall figure hides important geographical variations. Some local authorities saw significant increases: in Merthyr Tydfil the number of homelessness applications rose by 29% in the year to 2019-2020, with 807 households having applied for assistance. Similarly, there were increases in Swansea (+18%, to 3,060 households) and Carmarthenshire (+13%, to 2,346 households), and Powys Newport and Rhondda Cynon Taf all saw 11% increases (699, 2,235 and 1,653 households respectively).

The biggest reductions in applications were observed in South East Wales, with a 38% fall in 2019-2020 compared to 2018-2019 in Torfaen (down to 774 households) and a decrease of 24% in Monmouthshire (to 459 households). Other areas that saw a decrease include Caerphilly (-14% to 1800 households), Isle of Anglesey (-12% to 594), and Flintshire (-10% to 1,203).

There were no changes in Cardiff, which remains the area with the highest number of homelessness applications (5,598 households, or 36 out of every 1,000 households living in Cardiff).

Behind the homelessness applications figures, there are two other aspects that deserve closer attention.

First, local authorities in Wales were increasingly more likely to be providing assistance to households experiencing homelessness than to those whose homelessness could be prevented.

In April 2019-March 2020 in Wales, the number of households receiving assistance due to being at risk of experiencing homelessness within 56 days decreased by 7% to 9,993 households compared to 2018-2019. On the contrary, the number of households assessed as already experiencing homelessness increased by 6% to 12,399 households. Similarly, the number of households assessed as unintentionally experiencing homelessness and being in priority need increased by 16% to 3,060 households.

We observed a similar relative increase in relief support compared to prevention support in England. Here, the increase of +4% of homelessness applications in 2019-2020 compared to 2018-2019 has been driven by a +14.9% increase in the number of cases to support households experiencing homelessness. On the other hand, prevention support remained stable.

It seems possible this trend has continued in Wales post March 2020 given the scale of emergency support provided during the

Chart 4: Households in temporary accommodation, at 31 March, by type (a) (b) (c) (d)

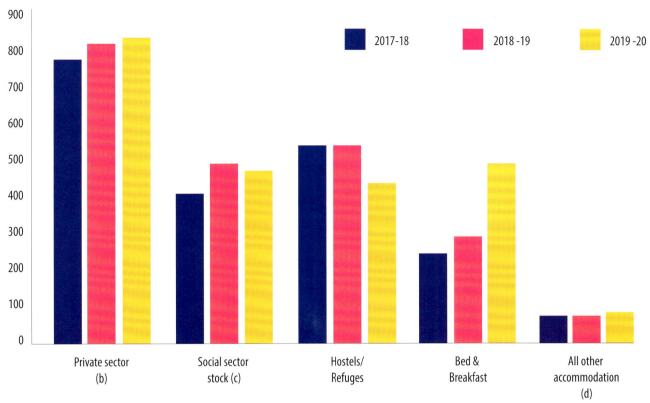

(a) Under the Housing (Wales) Act 2014
(b) Includes households placed directly with a private sector accommodation leased by local authorities and private sector accommodation leased by registered social landlords
(c) Includes local authority stock and registered social landlord
(d) 'Other' accommodation type includes homeless at home

Source: Statutory Homelessness data collection from local authorities

pandemic. In England, official statistics reveal a sharp -34.6% decrease in prevention duties in April-June 2020 compared to January-March 2020, against a +1.6% increase in relief duties.

What is clear from these figures is that crisis responses are dominating the statutory picture but efforts to tackle homelessness extend beyond these official figures. Local areas no doubt will want to keep a close eye on this trend and try to identify opportunities to reverse this trend so they are able to prevent homelessness from happening in the first place – i.e. before applicants' circumstances force them into the statutory system.

The long-lasting economic impact of the current pandemic is putting more people at risk of experiencing homelessness. Given the detrimental long-term effects of homelessness on people's lives, but also on public spending, it is paramount that we focus more effort on preventing homelessness to occur in the first place.

Second, households in temporary accommodation were more likely to be accommodated in B&Bs than in the private rented sector. There was an increase of 4% to 2,324 in TA placements in the period in question. This increase was driven by a +68% increase in the number of households accommodated in B&B accommodation. This increase was particularly marked over March 2020 which is possibly due to the COVID-19 pandemic and a shift in practice: some

households have been accommodated although they would ordinarily not have had an emergency accommodation duty. On the other hand, the number of households housed in hostels or refuges decreased.

If we are to move towards an evidence-led end to homelessness it is essential that we make use of all the homelessness data made available to us by local and national government. Analysing the year on year changes in homelessness statistics, noting regional differences and drilling down into the shifting picture of both the causes and effects of homelessness is a crucial part of understanding what works.

26 October 2020

First published on homelessnessimpact.org on 26 October 2020. Please see homelessnessimpact.org and the Welsh Government website for the most up-to date information.

Rough sleeping snapshot in England: autumn 2020

Statistical release about the annual single night snapshot of the number of people sleeping rough in local authorities across England.

Ministry of Housing, Communities & Local Government 25 February 2021

Details

The annual rough sleeping snapshot provides information about the estimated number of people sleeping rough on a single night between 1 October and 30 November each year and some basic demographics details (age, gender, nationality). These statistics provide a way of estimating the number of people sleeping rough across England on a single night and assessing change over time.

Local authorities across England take an annual autumn snapshot of rough sleeping using either a count-based estimate of visible rough sleeping, an evidence-based estimate meeting with local partners, or an evidence-based estimate meeting including a spotlight count in specific areas. This methodology has been in place since 2010. The snapshot is collated by outreach workers, local charities and community groups and is independently verified by Homeless Link.

Things you need to know

♦ People sleeping rough are defined as those sleeping or about to bed down in open air locations and other places including tents and make shift shelters.

♦ The snapshot can take place on a single date chosen by the local authority between 1 October to 30 November

♦ The snapshot records only those people seen, or thought to be, sleeping rough on a single night in autumn each year.

♦ The snapshot does not include people in hostels or shelters, people sofa surfing or those in recreational or organised protest, those in squats or traveller campsites.

♦ The snapshot process and figures are independently verified by Homeless Link.

♦ The snapshot can be carried out using either a count-based estimate, an evidence-based estimate meeting with local partners or an evidence-based estimate with spotlight count.

♦ The snapshot is collated by outreach workers, local charities and community groups.

♦ The snapshot does not include everyone in an area with a history of sleeping rough, or everyone sleeping rough in between October to November.

♦ The snapshot methodology which includes all local authorities has been in place since 2010, before only a quarter of areas did a snapshot.

♦ Accurately estimating the number of people sleeping rough is difficult given the hidden nature of rough sleeping.

How can it be used?

✓ To estimate the number of people sleeping rough on a single night in autumn

✗ To estimate the total number of people sleeping rough across the year

✓ To assess changes in the number of people sleeping rough over time

✗ To estimate the total number of homeless people

✓ To compare local authorities and regions in England

✗ To compare with other countries in the UK

✓ To understand some basic characterstics about people who sleep rough

✗ To understand how long people sleep rough and the reasons why people sleep rough

Rough sleeping snapshot in England: autumn 2020

The snapshot provides a way of estimating the number of people sleeping rough across England on a single night.

2,688
People sleeping rough on a single night in autumn 2020

37% decrease since last year

52% increase since 2010

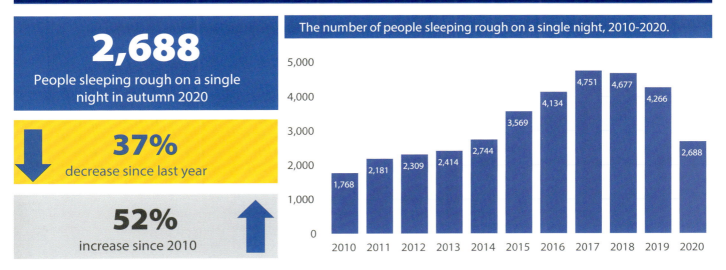

The number of people sleeping rough on a single night, 2010-2020.

Year	Number
2010	1,768
2011	2,181
2012	2,309
2013	2,414
2014	2,744
2015	3,569
2016	4,134
2017	4,751
2018	4,677
2019	4,266
2020	2,688

Nearly half (44 %) of all people sleeping rough on a single night in autumn are in London and the South East.

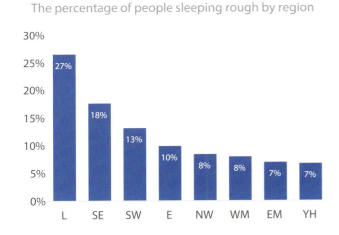

The percentage of people sleeping rough by region

L 27% · SE 18% · SW 13% · E 10% · NW 8% · WM 8% · EM 7% · YH 7%

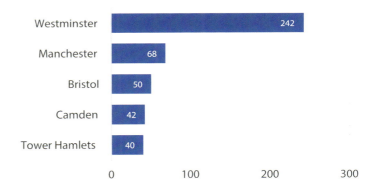

Local authorities with the highest estimated number of people sleeping rough

Local authority	Number
Westminster	242
Manchester	68
Bristol	50
Camden	42
Tower Hamlets	40

The snapshot collects some basic demographic information about those people found sleeping rough.

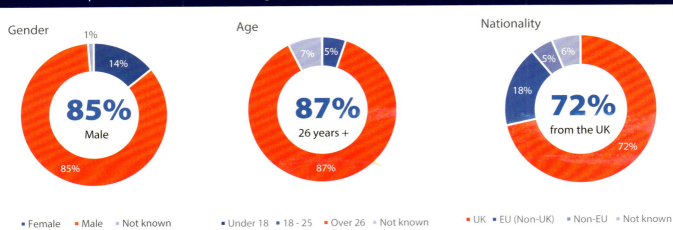

Gender — 85% Male · 14% · 1%

■ Female ■ Male ■ Not known

Age — 87% 26 years + · 7% · 5%

■ Under 18 ■ 18 - 25 ■ Over 26 ■ Not known

Nationality — 72% from the UK · 18% · 5% · 6%

■ UK ■ EU (Non-UK) ■ Non-EU ■ Not known

Statistical release is available here: https://www.gov.uk/government/collections/homelessness-statistics#rough-sleeping

Youth homelessness has risen 40% in five years, says UK charity

Centrepoint estimates 121,000 homeless or at risk, with analysis showing black people disproportionately affected.

By Aamna Mohdin and Tobi Thomas

Youth homeless in the UK has increased by an estimated two-fifths in five years, rising to more than 120,000, a leading charity director has warned, as fresh analysis suggests that black households are likely to be disproportionately affected

Seyi Obakin, the chief executive of Centrepoint, the UK's leading youth homelessness charity, said its estimates show 86,000 young people in the UK presented to their local authority as homeless or at risk in 2016/17, and that the figure increased to 121,000 in 2019-20.

Obakin expressed fears that youth homelessness would worsen as a result of the pandemic, with Centrepoint's helpline receiving a record number of calls since the start of the crisis. He also believes young black Britons will probably be disproportionately affected.

His warnings come as *Guardian* analysis shows that although England's black population stands at about 3.5%, black households make up 10% of those that are homeless or at risk of homelessness, according to data from the Department for Levelling Up, Housing and Communities (DLUHC) for the year 2020-21.

Youth homelessness

In London, black households represent 30% of those owed homelessness prevention or homelessness relief by their local authorities, despite making up just 12.5% of London's population.

In the Guardian analysis, homelessness, and being at risk of homelessness, is defined by whether a local authority owes prevention or relief duty to a household. The data is not broken down by age.

'It is not surprising that black households are overrepresented in official homelessness statistics, but this does not mean we should tolerate it. Without a home, children's development and educational attainment suffers and it becomes harder to find a job or stay healthy or maintain relationships that enable people to thrive,' Obakin said.

Obakin said that Centrepoint saw a third more calls to the helpline since the start of the pandemic, with huge surges of demand around local lockdowns. He pinned this increase down to the multiple crisis disproportionately affecting young people, from mental health issues to high unemployment, and urged the government to intervene.

'The problem is worse than it was a decade ago and it's actually worse than it was two years ago,' Obakin said. 'It is heartbreaking to see the range of complex issues that young people are presenting with is also getting wider. That in a way is a mirror of what's happening in society itself.'

He said racial disparities in youth unemployment, with Guardian analysis showing black youth employment was more than three times higher than among their white counterparts, had a knock-on effect on youth homelessness. 'We know from our data that about three-fifths of young people who seek help from Centrepoint are from ethnically diverse backgrounds,' he added.

Ethnic breakdown

He fears the problem will worsen now the government has pushed ahead with its planned cuts to universal credit, which he describes as a vital safety net. 'That safety net is what is being cut. So I worry young black people will be disproportionately affected,' he said.

Obakin said that through the newly created DLUHC, the government has a 'tremendous opportunity' to not only tackle rough sleeping, 'but to go beyond and ensure that those who are homeless, or face homelessness, are given the support and services they need before they have to sleep rough. That is good for the people, and it is also good for the taxpayer.'

A DLUHC spokesperson said: 'The government is helping prevent more young people from becoming homeless, and this year we've invested £750 million to tackle homelessness and rough sleeping.

'During the pandemic we made huge progress to bring rough sleepers off the streets, helping over 37,000 people into safe and secure accommodation, including 26,000 who have already moved into longer-term accommodation.'

18 October 2021

Understanding youth homelessness

Causes of youth homelessness

According to the latest Scottish Government statistics, there were 8,319 young people registered as homeless in Scotland in 2019/2020. This is a concerning figure as it represents almost 26% of the entire Scottish homeless population, even though young people only make 12% of the nation's total population!

Understanding youth homelessness

It is important to remember that there are many forms of homelessness, some of them can be very visible such as rough sleeping, others include circumstances where people are living in temporary accommodation (hostels, B&B). However, homelessness also includes what is referred to as hidden homelessness, where young people stay in unsuitable or insecure accommodation, or sofa-surfing with family or friends.

The homelessness route is a negative and stigmatising experience for young people, and it should be avoided whenever possible by early intervention programmes, mediation with the families, suitable affordable accommodation and early-on advice and support.

Youth homelessness is different from adult homelessness and services should recognize that difference. Age, in fact, matters for many reasons. Young people are transitioning from childhood to adulthood, meaning that their emotional, cognitive and social skills are still developing. These developments will normally be supported by adult supervision and support, both at home and outside.

Unfortunately, young people who become homeless do not fully experience the process of adolescent development, thus leaving home without the necessary skills, the financial support or the experience in running a household. The lack of stability and security will have an impact on young people's mental and physical health, increasing their chances of being exploited, abused or involved in criminal activities. Furthermore, homelessness can disrupt their education and it will significantly lower their possibilities of finding and keeping a job.

Extensive research highlights that young people with experience of care, from the LGBT community and with ACEs are currently overrepresented within the homelessness community and they are at an increased risk of experiencing homelessness.

Three main causes consistently make almost 70% of all applications

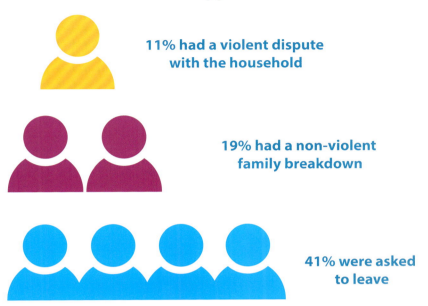

11% had a violent dispute with the household

19% had a non-violent family breakdown

41% were asked to leave

Our youth homelessness prevention pathways, commissioned by the Homelessness Prevention and Strategy Group, will support the implementation of the Ending Homelessness Together Action Plan and present recommendations to end youth homelessness in Scotland.

What does homelessness mean?

Under the Housing (Scotland) Act 1987 a person should be treated as homeless, even if they have accommodation, if it would not be reasonable for them to continue to stay in it.

Homelessness does not mean roofless and you do not have to be living on the street to be considered homeless. You could be staying with family or friends, or be living in an unsuitable accommodation, and you could still be assessed as homeless.

Rough sleeper numbers 'down a third in a year' but charities warn figures do not show full extent

Charities warned that the number of recorded rough sleepers is 'a significant underestimate of the true scale of homelessness'.

By Gabriella Swerling, Social and Religious Affairs Editor

The number of rough sleepers has fallen by more than a third in a year, government data shows, but shows an increase of 52 per cent since 2010.

The Ministry of Housing, Communities and Local Government (MHCLG) has released data showing that the number of people estimated to be sleeping rough on a single night in autumn has fallen by more than a third in a year.

There were 2,688 people estimated to be sleeping rough on a single night in autumn 2020 in England. This was a decrease of 1,578 people (37 per cent) from 2019.

However, it also marked a 52 per cent increase since 2010 when there were 1,768 rough sleepers. This was also the year in which the Government first began recording the number of rough sleepers using the 'snapshot' approach to data collection.

Responding to the figures, published in the Annual Rough Sleeping Count, charities warned that the number of rough sleepers recorded by the Government is 'a significant underestimate of the true scale of homelessness' and is 'just the tip of the iceberg'.

The Government's 'snapshot' method involves counting the number of rough sleepers on a single given night in the autumn in each local authority area.

Polly Neate, chief executive of Shelter, said: 'The huge effort made to help people off the streets shows what can be done. But the war is not won. No one should be sleeping rough during the pandemic, and we're still a long way from zero.

'Emergency accommodation needs to be there for everyone at risk of the street, yet we know it's not. Every week our frontline services pick up new cases of homeless people who are being point blank refused any help.

'Just one of the cases we've dealt with involved a frightened young man who was turned away no less than four times by the council in the dead of winter, because they said he wasn't in 'priority need'.

'Whether someone is offered a safe bed for the night instead of a cold pavement, should not be up for debate.

'The pandemic isn't over, and we must continue to keep people safe. The Government needs to ensure its hard work is not undone by giving councils explicit guidance to provide everyone with emergency accommodation and support.'

The Salvation Army also warned that the Government figures showing a drop in rough sleepers across England could be masking 'a surge in hidden homelessness'.

Lorrita Johnson, The Salvation Army's director of homelessness services, said: 'Any official figures that suggest fewer people are being forced to sleep rough offer a glimmer of hope.'

However, she added: 'The Government can't keep guessing about the number of rough sleepers, and a more robust recording method is needed so that funding can be properly allocated to cover the costs local councils are facing for homelessness support.'

Local authorities said the 37 per cent decrease in rough sleepers was due to the Government's 'Everyone In' scheme, where councils were instructed to rapidly rehouse thousands of rough sleepers at the start of the Covid-19 pandemic, as well as its Rough Sleeping Initiative which launched in 2018.

In 2018, the Government recorded 4,677 rough sleepers in its annual count. The following year, it recorded 4,266 and by autumn 2020 (just months after the launch of the 'Everyone In' campaign) the figure fell to 2,688.

As a result, charities warned that the annual count in November 2020 happened during the 'Everyone In' initiative when 9,866 people were already temporarily housed in emergency accommodation, including hotels. Therefore, anyone counted for the new Government figures is likely to be newly homeless or had returned to the streets.

The MHCLG said a range of factors should be considered when comparing the annual snapshots, including: the weather, movement across local authority boundaries, the date and time of the snapshot, and availability of night shelters.

Housing Secretary Rt Hon Robert Jenrick MP said, 'Ending rough sleeping is a personal mission for the Prime Minister and me – and we have made huge progress since he came into No.10 reducing rough sleeping by 43%. There is more to do, but I am determined to continue to drive progress forward backed by £750 million in funding.

'Government statistics on the rough sleeper count say that unlike last year, the ongoing 'Everyone In' scheme has helped to protect thousands of vulnerable people during the Covid-19 pandemic, including those sleeping rough or at risk of sleeping rough.'

'By November, the scheme had supported around 33,000 people with nearly 10,000 currently in emergency accommodation and over 23,000 already moved on into longer- term accommodation since the pandemic began.'

25 February 2021

Reports of rough sleeping in UK rose sharply during lockdown

Exclusive: increase came despite government claim 90% of homeless people had been helped off streets.

By Sarah Marsh and Niamh McIntyre

Reports of people sleeping rough rose sharply during lockdown, despite claims by government that more than 90% of homeless people had been helped off the streets at the height of the pandemic, the Guardian can reveal.

While the government launched a multimillion pound scheme to rehouse people during the Coronavirus crisis, charities said the pandemic had also led to a new cohort of people being made homeless as the services and facilities that they normally relied on closed.

Many were forced on to the streets when they lost jobs as the economy closed down, with those who did not have access to public funds – such as some foreign nationals – particularly affected.

The government's Everyone In scheme – which saw £3.2 million spent on getting people off the streets and into accommodation – was held up as an example of what could be done when homelessness was made a priority. Housing, communities and local government secretary Robert Jenrick boasted they had successfully taken 90% of rough sleepers off the streets to protect them from the virus.

However, new figures from the homelessness charity Streetlink show the picture was a more complicated one. Alerts by members of the public about rough sleepers increased by 36% year on year between April and June 2020, reaching 16,976. Notifications were also higher than the previous quarter which is unusual as they tend to rise in winter months, charities said.

The rise was particularly pronounced in the capital where there was a 76% increase, making up 71% of all alerts, substantially higher than usual. This is mirrored by annual figures on rough sleepers seen by outreach workers, published by the Greater London Authority, which showed numbers up by a third compared to the same period last year.

Matt Harrison, director of Streetlink, said the rise in reports could have been, in part, because rough sleepers were more visible during lockdown because streets were quieter, and that members of the public had heightened concern. But he also said that new people are being 'forced to sleep rough for the first time as a direct impact of the virus' as support services shut.

'We know that more people sleeping rough were calling us because they were concerned about the pandemic situation and weren't sure where to turn, particularly as the services and facilities that they normally relied on – including homelessness day centres, community centres and public toilets – had closed,' he said.

The Everyone In scheme, launched in March by Jenrick, gave emergency funding to help rough sleepers self-isolate in hotels and other housing during the height of the pandemic. It allowed healthcare and addiction services in some cases to engage with people who had long refused any help.

The government has repeatedly claimed that 90% of rough sleepers were helped during the pandemic. But, in June, the Office for Statistics Regulation criticised ministers for a lack of transparency by quoting figures without publishing supporting data.

Glen Bramley, professor of urban studies at Heriot-Watt University, said that government data on rough sleeping was based on an estimate of street counts which was 'not a reliable system'. He said the actual number of rough sleepers could be much higher than official statistics suggest.

He said that we were 'never going to see a disappearance of rough sleeping [after the introduction of the Everyone In scheme] due to the fact that there is always turnover in the population and people moving in and out of the situation'.

Bramley said: 'One thing happened when lockdown happened was that a large number of people who were in

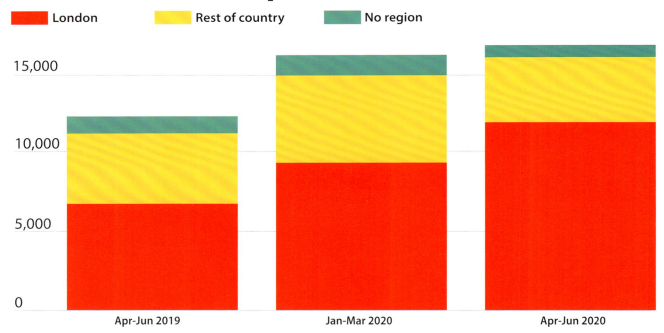

There were 16,976 alerts made by the public about rough sleepers between April and June 2020

Legend: **London** (red), **Rest of country** (yellow), **No region** (green)

Y-axis: 15,000 / 10,000 / 5,000 / 0

X-axis: Apr-Jun 2019 · Jan-Mar 2020 · Apr-Jun 2020

Source: Streetlink. Note: No region allocated when alert has no location or is a call asking for advice

the self-employment sector or on zero-hours contracts, or in informal employment situations – many of them migrants – immediately lost all work and ability to pay rent, so some of those people would be feeding into the new street homeless population.'

The data from Streetlink comes as charities warn that the homelessness problem is likely to get worse in the coming months if the government pushes ahead with a plan to lift a ban on evictions on 23 August, which is currently supporting those who have fallen behind on their rent.

Data obtained by the Guardian also suggests that just a fraction of those given shelter through the Everyone In scheme have been permanently rehoused and that hundreds were evicted from their hotel rooms due to antisocial behaviour. Charities warned that those evicted from the scheme will have returned to the streets and would be vulnerable in a second wave of the virus during the winter months.

Data obtained by freedom of information requests to 21 councils, including London boroughs and five other major cities across England, shows that of the nearly 4,000 people they housed under the scheme between March and May, 1,000 had left by the end of that period. The figures came from 16 London councils, Leicester, Bristol, City of Leeds, Coventry and Bradford.

16 councils of the 21 councils to provide figures gave a breakdown for the reason for early departure. Of the 3,246 housed by those local authorities, only 11% have gone on to be rehoused, while 5% were asked to leave because of antisocial behaviour.

Caroline Bernard, head of policy and communications at Homeless Link, said: 'Our members reported that although they have successfully engaged many entrenched rough sleepers during the pandemic who had previously refused

support, some people chose not to remain in their emergency accommodation.

'Many of these individuals struggled with isolation, social distancing and disruption to their support network and access to treatment, and returned to rough sleeping. However, services continue to support them and look for more sustainable housing solutions.'

She added that while the government scheme was appreciated there were concerns that it may exclude people with no access to public funds, and included no specialist provision for women, young people and survivors of domestic abuse.

An MHCLG spokesperson said: 'The government has taken unprecedented action to support the most vulnerable people in our society during the pandemic – backed by over half a billion pounds to tackle homelessness and rough sleeping this year and next.

'Nearly 15,000 vulnerable people have been housed in emergency accommodation and we are funding longer-term accommodation – 3,300 homes this year alone – and tailored support so as few people as possible return to life on the streets.'

18 August 2020

'I didn't shower for 2 months': what it's like being homeless in London during a pandemic

Coffee shops closed, shelters in limited supply, and a beacon of hope from hotel accommodation - two Londoners share their stories.

By Rachael Davis, Features Editor

The wider impact of the pandemic has pushed more Londoners into homelessness, unable to stay safe and stay at home during lockdown. It goes without saying that the pandemic has not been easy for any of us.

But while most Londoners followed lockdown instructions to stay at home, many didn't have that luxury.

In fact, for London's homeless population, life got even tougher than before.

The lifelines many relied on, like coffee shops for WiFi to look for work, soup kitchens for a hot meal, and busy streets for small acts of kindness from the public all disappeared overnight as lockdown came into force.

'Before the pandemic hit in March we had seen the highest numbers of people rough sleeping in the capital since figures started being recorded - a 21 per cent increase on the previous year,' said Ruth Jacob, senior policy officer at homelessness charity Crisis.

'We have seen an extraordinary effort from the Government's 'Everyone In' initiative to get people safely into accommodation during the pandemic, as well as efforts from the Mayor's Office, local authorities and charities in London, so huge numbers of people have been helped into safe accommodation.

'But we have continued to see more people being pushed into homelessness, and I think that's really down to the wider impact of the pandemic as people have lost their jobs, lost income.'

Ruth said that there are huge structural problems in London which hinder the ending of homelessness in the capital, not least the high cost of living.

However, as two former rough sleepers told *MyLondon*, the use of hotels as short term accommodation for homeless

people throughout the pandemic has given many the boost they need to get off the streets for good.

Joshua's story

Joshua (not his real name), 42, now works as an assistant in radiology at Ealing Hospital. Joshua originally came from a stable background and upbringing, working in compliance for a decade leading up to the 2008 financial crash.

He told *MyLondon* that the financial crash was a low point in his life, but things got lower from then. In 2016, Joshua hit rock bottom - debts, failed businesses and strained family relationships were taking their toll.

He checked into a hotel, keen to leave the family environment hoping things might improve, but they didn't.

Joshua said: 'To be more resourceful with my savings, I traded a comfortable life for the side streets of Charing Cross. A world away from the life I once had.'

The winter of 2016 was tough. Bitterly cold, fearing for his safety and at a loss for what else to do, one night Joshua boarded a night bus to Heathrow Airport hoping he would find some shelter.

He said: 'It's practically the only place that's open 24 hours.

'For a while, it became a routine to sleep on the plastic chairs at the terminal, pretending to be a passenger leaving early morning.

'That became a habit for three and a half years.'

Joshua would use the WiFi in coffee shops and hotel lobbies to look for work every day before returning to the airport at night.

'I became rudderless, lacking clear sense, moving from terminal to terminal, hotel lobby to hotel lobby and, at times, stretching out time on bus routes,' he said.

In March 2020, when lockdown was announced, the places Joshua used every day were closing. He never used to spend the daytimes in the airport, but one day he decided he had no other choice but to spend the day in the terminal waiting room.

Almost by fate, on that day there was an outreach team in the airport who were approaching people they knew were homeless.

Joshua said: 'I noticed they were going round, I approached them, explained my situation, and they referred me to the Travelodge hotel in Aldgate.

'When I got to the Travelodge I met the team from St Mungo's [homeless charity]. St Mungo's have been a welcome blessing, and the comfort of the hotel was a relief.

'After a long time I was free of one less worry.

'Not that there weren't other concerns: I was troubled by my lack of clothes or how long the accommodation would be for. But these too were taken care of by the lovely staff, a wide range of clothes provided along with other essentials, and assurance that they will do what they can to find a suitable future place.'

Joshua went from surviving off one meal a day while living in the airport to being served three meals a day at the hotel. He praised Red Radish catering company, which usually caters for touring crews for festivals and film sets, but had been working with St Mungo's and the Mayor of London on their hotels for the homeless project during the coronavirus crisis.

Joshua spent April to August of 2020 living at the hotel, where he had the luxury of books, TV, paints and other sources of entertainment. He also got into running and cycling, enjoying the quiet London streets at the peak of lockdown.

Staying in the hotel meant Joshua had an address to use to apply for jobs and other forms of support. Thanks to a glowing reference from St Mungo's, he was able to get a job at Ealing Hospital as an assistant in radiology. He was also able to secure a set of keys to a place he can call his own.

He said: 'The carriage on the underground is probably bigger, but whichever way you look at it, it's a place and a stable roof over me to rebuild myself.

'It means so much - that one of the first acts I carried out was to walk around, give thanks to the walls, roof, and decorations. I paused to give gratitude to the safety this new place will provide.

'The speed at which my life has changed since the pandemic feels so surreal. The shift from stagnation to flow is an amazing feeling to have. The team at St Mungo's see beyond someone's homeless status, taking notice, providing plenty of support and giving hope.'

Joshua has his current, privately-rented home on a year-long contract with the option to renew. His job offers career progression, and after a year he could become a radiologist technician.

In many ways, the pandemic itself led directly to Joshua getting the support he needed to get off the streets

'Sometimes in chaos, opportunity arises,' he said.

Roland's story

Roland, 34, now lives in a council-funded hostel in Southall, West London. Just a few months ago he was sleeping rough on the streets in the middle of a global pandemic.

Roland came to London at the end of the summer after losing his place in accommodation in Cardiff. He admitted he was breaking lockdown rules in order to see his then-partner, which cost him his home and job as a cleaner in the building he lived in.

He then tried to find accommodation that would house both him and his partner, but found none available for couples, forcing them both onto the streets.

They were living on the streets of Cardiff for months, surviving solely on Roland's then-partner's Universal Credit payment of £380 per month.

Roland could not claim Universal Credit himself, as there had been complications with his application and he had lost some essential ID pertaining to his immigration status while moving through the homelessness system.

This meant that when he came to London after breaking up with his partner - a break-up caused by the strain of trying to survive a pandemic on the streets - he was left with no income whatsoever.

Roland said: 'It was really hard. I went to food banks and soup kitchens, but I'd say about 90 per cent of them are shut at the moment.

'You have to walk a long, long distance from your sleeping spot to the place. But when you get to the food bank there's another problem - even if you get quite a lot of food, they give you enough for a week, where do you put it?

'You have to carry it, because if you hide it someone will find it, either other homeless people or cleaners who think it is just rubbish and put it in the bin.

'It puts you in a mindset just to survive.'

Roland said that there was a period where he was unable to shower for two months, because the usual places he would use to maintain personal hygiene were closed for the lockdown.

Similarly, he struggled to find places to charge his phone - a lifeline when you're living on the streets.

Prior to lockdown, libraries were a haven for phone charging and access to the internet to look for work and shelter. He tried everything from random plugs in shopping centres to sockets in churches, gradually getting moved on from one place to the next by security guards.

Eventually, Roland's luck began to turn. The first beacon of hope was a hotel room offered over Christmas, as part of an initiative by Crisis.

Crisis senior policy officer Ruth Jacob said: 'Every year Crisis runs a huge "Crisis at Christmas" operation across London that helps people who are rough sleeping with a place to stay for usually a week over Christmas, but this year it was extended because of the situation.

'It helps to make sure that people have a safe and happy Christmas, but also to link people to ongoing services that can help make sure they can move on to settled accommodation.

'We were able to provide two weeks of hotel accommodation, access to healthcare, and crucially access to advice.'

This help from Crisis helped Roland get off the streets for two weeks at Christmas. He said: 'It was really useful, there were many benefits to it.

'The place itself was lovely - it was located in Crystal Palace, but it was great to have somewhere to go back to and to keep out of the cold.

'It was great to have clothing, that was nice, and they would bring us any necessities we needed.'

After the two weeks in the hotel, Roland had to sleep rough for another couple of days. But then, in perfect timing, he was finally granted settled status after living in the UK for 12 years since moving from his home country of Hungary.

This meant his lost identification was no longer a problem, as his settled status meant a proof letter could be generated for any authority in lieu of ID. Within a couple of days, the council got in touch to offer him a place to stay in Southall.

Roland now has a place to live where he can finally get a replacement passport and start applying for jobs. He has his eye on some recruitment agencies, as he says the demand for warehouse workers is huge.

Simply having a roof over his head means he can work on staying off the streets and rebuilding his life.

26 January 2021

www.mylondon.news

A personal story of hidden homelessness and its circular relationship with mental health

By Ed Brown

Homelessness is such an everyday injustice that it becomes normalised, figuring as a morality tale of mistakes made and consequences for the workshy or deviant. A dismal reality that is easily disregarded through a quick averting of gaze or a half-hearted fumbling through your pockets only to reply, 'Sorry, mate'. However, in reality for most of us, homelessness is too close for comfort, as it is potentially only a few bills and months away, or as Amelia's story shows is often connected to the chances of our own personal throw of the dice and being incapacitated by mental ill-health.

Rough sleeping has been on the rise in recent years; stats published this week by the Office for National Statistics revealed that rough sleeping for a single night in England increased 168.7% from 2010 to a height in 2017, only to decrease slightly in 2018 and 2019 and then to dramatically decrease in 2020 by 43.4% from the 2017 peak.

The 2020 estimate suggests that the government's £3.2 million 'Everyone In' initiative response to the pandemic was a success. However momentary, it was a reprieve from living on the streets or in insecure temporary accommodation.

Responding to the ONS figures, Nat Travis, national head of substance misuse at Turning Point, commented: 'In a civilised society, nobody should need to sleep on the streets. The increase in numbers of the past ten years is a poor reflection on our society. The 'Everyone In' initiative is a real success story which is reflected in the numbers going down over the last year; however, there is still much more to be done.'

'We must look past the numbers and recognise that there are thousands of real people, some of them teenagers who are sleeping without a warm bed tonight. More must be done to tackle the root causes of homelessness – precarious housing and employment, debt, family breakdown and drug and alcohol and mental health problems', he added.

Amelia's story of mental health, homelessness, and securing a future

In a self-feeding cycle, people experiencing mental health problems are more susceptible to becoming homeless, and the stresses of becoming homeless are more likely to amplify poor mental health. This was represented by a 2014 study, which found that 80% of homeless people in England reported that they had mental health issues and 45% that they had been diagnosed with a mental health condition.

According to the most recent ONS data, the vast majority of people rough sleeping in England and Scotland (80%) are males, with an overall ratio of six men to one woman. Although, as campaigners told Mental Health Today in March, this does not reveal the complete picture of homelessness, as while women are largely absent from the more visible injustices of living on the street, women are more likely to be 'invisibly homeless', and rely on means such as sofa surfing.

One such woman, Amelia Davidson, 28, spoke with Mental Health Today about her experience of facing homelessness, mental health, and navigating the housing system.

Amelia said that her life changed 'dramatically' after losing both her parents; the bereavement of losing two figures of stability in her life triggered feelings of anxiety and depression, for which she seeks regular counselling to cope with her pain, suffering, and loss.

'I miss their company and the fact that they were always there for me whatever went wrong. Now I feel very lonely and on my own.'

After renewed struggles with her mental health, Amelia commented that she felt as if she had been 'thrown into the deep end', and the thought of maintaining a 9-5 job in a pressured environment felt too much while coping with substantial levels of grief, anxiety, and depression.

Falling through the cracks, Amelia had to navigate finding a place after losing her home. She said that from her experience, 'the housing system is not always as helpful as it could be… There is a set of criteria to try to help the highest priority first, but everyone's story is unique and does not always fit into the criteria you have set out. The human aspect is missing from the system, a sympathetic ear has been replaced by a series of tick boxes, and if you do not tick the right ones, you get left behind. That needs to change.'

'This put me at the bottom of the list for housing and meant that I was only allowed to bid for 1-bedroom houses, but as most of those did not allow pets, and I refused to give up my dog, I was not eligible to bid for them. Being such a low priority anyway, I would not have been successful even if I had been eligible.'

She said that she had to rely on friends and family to help her stay off the streets, falling into the category of the many women who are hidden homeless. But once finding a home, Amelia is now again facing homelessness after recently receiving an eviction notice on her flat.

'I have been through so much heartache and trauma; all I want is to live a simple life doing the things that make me happy. I have learnt the hard way that you never know what is around the corner and that you need to go out and live your dreams, as you only get one chance.'

Ambitions for the future

Not lacking in the aspiration and determination to carve out a space for herself and make a difference in the lives of other women facing homelessness, Amelia wants to raise money to secure her future and find a place to call home that cannot be taken away from her.

'I have spent most of my life holding back from doing the things that make me happy due to living through these tough times and through fear of the unknown. Because of this, I am living in a pit of depression and anxiety, desperately clinging on to the hope that things will one day change.'

Hoping to turn several difficult years around by providing some stability, she intends to buy a plot of land where she would build a shepherd's hut for her and her dog, and then six additional huts to offer temporary accommodation for women, youth and those with pets facing homelessness.

Amelia said that she envisions it as a place that would create a community for those who have been struggling with homelessness to reconnect with the world and get back into a routine, which would enable them to transition into more stable housing placements and avoid falling back into the cycle of homelessness.

'My message to women who are experiencing similar circumstances would be to not be afraid to reach out for help. There are times when you feel alone and like the world is against you, and all you want to do is give up, but there is always someone out there who is willing to help. You just have to ask for it.'

11 June 2021

Callum's story

Callum, 23, left care at 18 and found a flat, but after some time the flat became unaffordable. After becoming homeless, his mental health then deteriorated to the point that he also lost his job. He used the Depaul UK Nightstop service before the charity offered him longer-term accommodation. With financial support from Depaul UK, he gained the qualifications needed to begin working for the fire service. His dream is to become a firefighter.

'As a young child I was in the care system. When I turned 18, I moved into my own flat, run by the local authority. I was on benefits, just scraping by. I did what I thought was the right thing to do and got a full-time job as a labourer. I was travelling from Oldham to Bury every day, getting up at 6am, getting to work for seven, working until half past four.

'Unfortunately, getting the job led to a spiral down. After a while, my rent went up and I couldn't afford it on my income. I thought the job was more important, so I left my flat. That's when I became homeless. I'd probably describe myself, at that time, as vulnerable. You've left a system where everything is in place for you, there's safety nets there. Then you've been cast out into a world where there's a lot to contend with.

'You're scared, but also brave. I remember the period before having to move out. I was thinking, 'Where am I going to go now? Where am I going to put all my belongings?' I stayed with mates, different people's sofas. As much as they have your best interests at heart, they get a bit sick of you. Eventually, you've used up all your options. With everything that was going on, my mental health wasn't in the best place, so that had an impact as well.

'I continued working for about four months after I left that flat. Having no fixed abode had an effect on me. I don't mind sharing it, my mental health at the time wasn't good. Quite a bit of depression. My employer laid me off, which meant I had to go back on benefits, which made the situation more difficult. It's like a snowball effect.

'My local housing group put me into contact with Depaul UK. They got me into Nightstop. I was very apprehensive because you're going to someone's house, you've never met them before. Then I met my Nightstop host and she helped me to settle in really quick. Such a lovely woman. It was nice to go home and have somewhere secure, safe. Last week, I was in Tesco and I noticed this lady. It was Helen, my Nightstop host. We gave each other a hug and she asked how I was doing. She was really happy, really pleased.

'After two weeks, Depaul UK sorted out my own flat. I was there for about a year and a half. While I was there I was volunteering with the Fire Service, full-time. A job came up with the Fire Service, a full-time, permanent role, and I got it!

'My next step is to go for full-time firefighter and I need to have my GCSE Maths and English to do that. At Depaul UK, I was told about a grant I could apply for, for education purposes. I went for the grant, for private tutoring, and I got the full amount. Thanks to Depaul. That's helped us as well.

'Ever since I was a little boy, I've always been really keen on helping people. I wanted to be a paramedic or a firefighter. Firefighting, it's not just rescuing people, it's the getting involved with your communities as well, supporting people who have been in the same situations as yourself. Giving back to society. I'm feeling good. The future is good, hopefully.'

Lyndsey - a personal journey

Through the Time for Change group, Lyndsey is using her experiences of homelessness to help others and to campaign for better services so that in the future people don't experience the same trauma that she's been through.

Lyndsey tells of a life history full of trauma, chaos and disruption. Unsurprisingly, she found coping strategies for what life put her way, but sometimes those strategies became unhealthy and overwhelming. At 16 she'd moved into her first homeless accommodation and by 38 she'd lived in over 25 different places. She experienced hostel after hostel, where some showed kindness and understanding but others were unsupportive, disapproving.

When Lyndsey's sister died from a heroin overdose, her life spiralled out of control, one more loss to the many lived through. She'd left a bad relationship, but life's pressures meant she wasn't able to keep her daughter with her. 'I hit rock bottom but there was no help. I was pre-judged – put in the box for 'has an alcohol problem' – and that was it.' That first night of renewed homelessness, Lyndsey went to an emergency shelter where her bed was a mattress on a church floor. She cried all night, contemplating everything that had led to this point in her life.

Lyndsey was then placed in a hostel on the edge of her local town, but this temporary accommodation only increased her emotional problems. 'It's an isolated building surrounded by woodland and it brought back horrible memories because I'd been assaulted in those woods once, but they wouldn't offer me anything else'.

Last Christmas Eve, Lyndsey received a phone call which left her crying uncontrollably. But it was a good call, news to say she had a permanent home and that she could move out of her hostel in the near future. A new beginning, a place for hope and a place to call hers. With support in place Lyndsey talks of her path to recovery and is doing well. 'I'm learning to be myself and also learning to stop punishing myself. My daughter's room is all unicorns. When I first moved in I just found myself walking around it because I was so used to just living in a single room for 9 and a half months. I just love my house.'

Her involvement with the Time for Change Edinburgh group has seen her visiting hostels pre lockdown and at its peak, she helped another peer handing out food to rough sleepers. With training from Shelter Scotland staff, Lyndsey is learning how to triage people looking for help with housing problems, with her own lived experience giving insight and awareness to current issues. 'You hear some horrific stories but it's really interesting and I love doing it. It's clear there's nowhere near enough housing.'

'Now I've got this great house I'm looking forward to having my daughter stay with me more. I've waited until she was ready. I've got a place where she can see herself living and I've rebuilt that trust. It means the world to me.'

Time for Change – answers from those who know the problem of homelessness best

Time for Change Edinburgh is a group for local people with lived experience of homelessness. The members of the group are known as peers. They use their own experiences to help Shelter Scotland decide what needs to change to improve services for people experiencing homelessness, and to help campaign for homelessness to stop altogether. Senior Development worker William Wright oversees Time for Change Edinburgh.

He said: 'The peers have helped me carry out research by talking to people using services for people who are struggling, places like temporary accommodation or food banks. We've found many people say there are issues with personal safety and mental health in temporary accommodation. Lyndsey became involved as a Time for Change peer in August 2019, and has helped local people, co-designed local responses, acquired qualifications, become a volunteer and has been involved in many other opportunities including partnership work with Margaret Mitchell.'

Working together to tell personal stories of significance

Working with people to tell aspects of their lives is something that Margaret Mitchell is committed to in her work as a photographer. The collaboration with the Time for Change network is part of her wider work 'An Ordinary Eden' which reflects upon the very human need to belong, to have security, to have stability. With the peer network and Shelter Scotland, she is working on photographs and stories from people with lived experience of homelessness. From initial discussions through to final selections, people choose what parts of their lives they want to share. Lyndsey's story is part of this work.

'Lyndsey and I have known each another for about a year now and I visited her in both temporary hostel accommodation and when she got permanent housing. I hope that by working together we can tell personal stories of significance.'

13 January 2021

John's story. 'The new limit on stays in temporary accommodation is incredible, it's going to change people's lives.'

By John, Edinburgh

'It was a surprise to me the way it all happened, when I became homeless. I lost my job in 2015 after a period of ill-health and had to apply for welfare benefits. I had been staying in a private rental since 2012 and in late 2018, the landlord decided to sell the flat and gave me two months' notice.

I was in a really difficult situation in the period of time between getting the notice and the end of the tenancy. I had no success in securing another private flat, due in part to my status as a Housing Benefit recipient. As soon as I was given notice, I went to Edinburgh Housing Advice Partnership who referred me to Crisis, who in turn advised me to contact the City of Edinburgh Council.

I went directly to the Council office and explained my situation, in short that I was going to be made homeless in two months time. Although I was given some information on the Council's procedure, I was told to come back and present as homeless on the day my tenancy ended. I couldn't believe it. That the Council declined to act despite the opportunity to do so was a missed opportunity to prevent a case of homelessness.

On the day my tenancy ended, I went back to the Council to present as homeless.

I sat and waited, then was called to an interview room and they said to me, "Okay we've got a spot in a B&B, there's nowhere else for you to go." I had no choice but to take it. That's how I ended up in unsuitable temporary accommodation for six months.

The place was filthy. There were cockroaches and vermin – I saw dead mice on a weekly basis. The shower drain backed up, so you'd end up ankle deep in dirty water. It had a kitchen but no fridge or freezer. The other residents took the pots and pans so there was nothing to cook with. My room was on the fourth floor, but the kitchen was on the first floor, and the only place to get water. I have mobility problems so going up and down three flights of stairs to get a drink was far from ideal.

I had a room to myself but there were heavy restrictions on what you could do. I had to leave the key when I left and be buzzed in when returning. There was a curfew. I couldn't spend a night away or stay with friends. The staff were often dismissive, unhelpful, and rude.

Last summer, I was accepted into the Crisis Help to Rent scheme. Even when applying through letting agents participating in the scheme, I was unable to find success. In many cases, letting agents on the scheme were not honouring the agreement they had made with Crisis. I was viewing about 10 flats a week, and applying for more but, again and again, was unable to get through the selection process and secure a tenancy.

I was a good candidate on paper. I have no history of rent arrears, anti-social problems or any other issues while maintaining private tenancies for many years, including when receiving Housing Benefit. I was able to provide an excellent reference from my previous letting agency, but this made no difference.

The Council put me on PSL (private sector leasing) list. After six months of being in the B&B, I was offered a flat. I went to view it and was told that the decision had be made then and there whether I should take it. I completed the paperwork

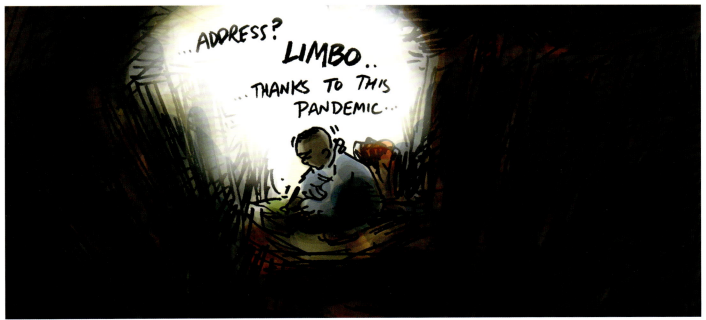

then and moved the next day. It was an easy decision. It wouldn't have taken much to be better than the B&B.

Living in the B&B was weird – it's like I just spent six months in survival mode. I wasn't really dealing with anything. I was just trying to get through each day. Having the flat has given me the relief of being able to live again – to be able to perform everyday tasks and exercise basic freedoms which I took for granted before my time in the B&B. I'm in a place with a door and a key that means I can come and go when I want. You really appreciate that, that makes a big difference. I'm able to store food, cook a meal. When I was in the B&B, I was always working out the cheapest way to get by, having to work around unhelpful restrictions, always thinking how I can not spend money. It makes no sense to house people already on a fixed income in such a way that they are forced to spend more than is necessary each day to meet their most basic needs.

Since moving into a flat I've had space and time to process what's happened to me. It shocked me how easy it is to become homeless – that I am homeless. I got very down and I'm still in the process of working through that. My accommodation situation is still uncertain – where I am is still classed as Temporary, and the bidding process for permanent housing is paused at the moment. The flat still does not feel quite like a home as a result.

The change in the law due to the virus is a great thing – I saw people who had been in the hostel a long time. It did nothing to help them really. There's nothing good about staying in those places long term, it affects you physically and mentally. Some people became so despondent that they just stayed in their rooms. It is such a dispiriting place to be.

The new limit on stays in temporary accommodation is incredible, it's going to change people's lives. Nobody should have to stay in a place like that for a long period of time. How are you meant to do anything without an address? How do you apply for a job, apply for a flat? It just makes getting on with your life more difficult than it needs to be.'

The swift action taken by Scottish Government to tackle homelessness during the pandemic include amendments made to the Unsuitable Accommodation Order. The changes equalise the law so that all people, not just families and pregnant women, in emergency accommodation must be rehoused into a more permanent home after 7 days. While many of us are experiencing isolation and restrictions for the first time as a result of the coronavirus outbreak, they can be common for people who are homeless. Feelings of fear, isolation, loneliness and desperation were identified in our research with people stuck in unsuitable temporary accommodation. But fast-tracking of this legislation should make these experiences a thing of the past. The changes to the Unsuitable Accommodation Order signal a win for our A Life in Limbo campaign. Launched in 2017, the campaign was in response to reports from our members and frontline staff, that people were languishing in unclean and unsafe accommodation for months and years on end.

Our homelessness stories - Shannon Kim Beecher, 23

Up until her sixth birthday, Shannon and her brother had lived in the care system. She settled in West Norwood after her adoptive parents, having originally planned on adopting one child, took in both siblings. But growing up for six years uncertain, unstable, and confused had eroded Shannon's mental health and sense of self-worth.

When Shannon was older, she was diagnosed with anxiety, depression, and anger issues because of her time in foster care, but as a child she didn't understand why she felt this way. Despite all of this, Shannon's relationship with her brother gave rise to her desire to put the needs of vulnerable people before her own. As a child, she refused to let anyone near her brother. She'd take him to the bathroom, tie his shoelaces, and hold his hand when he was upset. They were inseparable when they were in care.

'My mental health was never really diagnosed till I was an adult. They knew I had issues, but they never actually said what they thought they were.

'Growing up in foster care before the age of six can be traumatizing.'

'I always felt like such a bad kid for having all these anger issues, and then I looked back when I was much older and thought, 'no wonder I had anger issues! I realised I didn't know how to control it at that age and that I couldn't judge myself for that.'

Like other teenagers around her age, Shannon frequently fought with her adoptive parents, but it wasn't until they separated that things changed for the worse. At the time, Shannon worked for a learning disability and mental health charity. The stresses of home life began to compound with her work life, as she began to put the needs of others before her own again.

Shannon had always been a hard worker with a desire to help those that were vulnerable, but her good nature was taken advantage of. Her usual eight-hour shifts often turned to 10- or 12-hour shifts. She'd find herself walking home from work at 2am, exhausted and drained. She was the first one to say 'yes' to extra work, because she always wanted to help, but she suffered for it. Shannon ended up fainting on shift on more than one occasion and ultimately burnt out from the pressures at home and at work.

'Me and my mum didn't really get along. I wasn't able to keep a job because of my mental health and it was impacting my personality at home. It was never a pain for me to get a job, I could always get a job, which was really nice. I just couldn't keep it up because I was either overworking and running myself completely into the ground, or I would take on the emotional responsibility of everyone else around me.

'It was around this time that I left home. They never actually kicked me out, they just gave me a timeframe to leave and find my own place. They even let me have another month when I was struggling to find somewhere.'

Shannon decided to sofa surf at her friend's family home while she continued to look for a place, but that time was brief. Her friend had her own family issues and Shannon felt too uncomfortable to stay. Shannon became street homeless after failing to find housing through the council. She lacked a passport, provisional driver's licence, or the appropriate documents to support her application for housing, but she didn't give up. She remembers this period vividly and considers herself lucky despite her lived experiences.

'I ended up homeless for almost two months. It was horrendous, but when you meet the right people it can be alright. It's when you meet the wrong people that you can get into some trouble.

'Thankfully I didn't meet the wrong people. I met the nice people! Funnily enough, two of them I had known for years because every time I went to my local Sainsbury's I bought them something and they just remembered who I was. I remember them saying, 'You can't be the one that's here now!' They told me about all the places I could go to wash, eat or take shelter.'

'Whenever I go to that Sainsbury's I still buy them food to this day.'

During this difficult time, Shannon attributed her survival to finding safe places to sleep. She fell into a regular routine of sleeping during the day and staying awake during the night. There were times she took long trips on buses to find some peace in the chaos.

'There was one time I fell asleep on the 91 bus and the driver had noticed that I'd been on it for three trips. He actually bought me a sandwich and left it next to me. He didn't tell me to get off, or that I hadn't paid. He just let me sleep. I remember it being the first proper sleep I'd had in ages.'

'That act of kindness meant everything at the time.'

'I was so worried about falling asleep and something happening. It gave me hope that there was still kindness I could hold on to in humanity.'

After two months of being street homeless, Shannon finally hit a breakthrough with Lambeth council. Her case was pushed forward after Shannon's stepmother finally agreed to come in to verify Shannon's identity. After a few more weeks of moving between crash pads, churches and emergency housing offered by the council, she was referred to Evolve Housing + Support.

At first, Shannon was quiet and kept her distance from others, preferring to stay in her room. It took time and for a while she continued her routine of staying awake at night and sleeping in the day, but after a few more months Shannon began to engage with staff and counsellors.

In 2018, Evolve Housing + Support found a strong link between trauma, mental health and homelessness in its 'Hurt to Homelessness' report. Research revealed that 80% of homeless people have suffered a traumatic event in their childhood. The results highlighted the vital need for counselling and the pivotal impact it would have helping homeless people overcome their traumatic experiences and being able to move on.

By the time Shannon came to Evolve, the charity had launched a free, in-house counselling service for all homeless residents to help individuals break the cycle and achieve independence again. Speaking about her own experiences and her place in the world now, Shannon wanted people to know that the pathway to recovery is long but attainable.

'In the beginning I kept to myself. I didn't talk to anyone other than the staff, and even then it was only a few staff members. It took me a while to open up to anyone, even

my support worker at the time. My anxiety was really bad. I was in a brand new place with almost 100 other people and it felt really daunting after pretty much being by myself for ages.

'I actually went into hospital during my first year at Evolve. I thought I was doing well. I even managed to trick myself! I went to a play on the Southbank and my mates and I stayed out for a while. I remember we had a really nice evening, but half an hour after I got back to my room I took an overdose.

'It wasn't planned and looking back, it's clear I wasn't in a good place, but I managed to convince myself I was happy because I thought I should be.'

One of the biggest turning points for Shannon came when Manny joined the charity as a handyman and impromptu music teacher. Within the first few months of working with Evolve, Manny had set up a small music club to nurture the passion some young adults held for music at the homelessness service. Shannon joined the group to explore her own voice and today she recognises it as the day she found an outlet for some of her lived trauma.

'I'm still working on myself, but I've come so far.'

'I still do laundry at 3am because of my anxiety, but I've also opened myself up to so many more people and I feel so much more confident. Life has thrown a lot at me recently. Like, I know ten people alone in the last two months that have died and I'm trying to work through that with my counsellor. But the music lessons with Manny have been a huge help!

'I've learnt that if I want to be there for others, I need to look after myself first. Ever since I was child, I've tried to put others before myself, but it's always led to me crashing. I know if I want to look after vulnerable people in the future, I need to make sure I am looking after my own mental health, so I am around to do it.'

18 August 2021

Preventing labour exploitation of people facing homelessness

A blogpost.

By Anna Yassin, migrant project manager at Glass Door Homeless Charity

Based in London, Glass Door coordinates the UK's largest network of open-access services for people affected by homelessness. In an ordinary year, we provide a safe place to sleep for 175 people every night in our winter shelters. Our ability to assist is based on capacity not on eligibility criteria or local connection. We welcome people as guests, rather than as 'clients' or 'service users'. We offer respect and the idea that all people have dignity and value.

As a result of our open access policy, we meet people in particularly desperate situations, having been either rejected from services on grounds of eligibility, or too frightened and/or dejected by the requirements imposed to access the support they need. Among those are people who need a place to stay after leaving exploitation and/or who are waiting to be accommodated via the National Referral Mechanism (NRM), the UK's system to support people who have experienced modern slavery.

Issues faced by homeless survivors of modern slavery

Insecure housing is a key issue for survivors of modern slavery, as highlighted in a recently published report by Crisis. The research documented the experience of over 330 people from across the UK affected by homelessness and modern slavery over the past two years. Labour exploitation was identified as the second most common type of exploitation after sexual exploitation overall; however, it was the most prevalent type of exploitation among men

facing homelessness. It found that less than half (45%) of homeless survivors of modern slavery chose to enter the NRM, and that limited access to accommodation and legal advice is preventing survivors from seeking redress. It concluded that current government support for survivors is inadequate, leaving people trapped in homelessness and exposed to a risk of further exploitation.

These findings mirror what we see at Glass Door. Last winter, Glass Door caseworkers supported a number of guests escaping conditions of modern slavery. In one case, staff prevented entry into the hostel by someone looking for a guest who had left exploitation. The guest was kept safe and later accommodated via the NRM. Unfortunately, accommodation support is not guaranteed for survivors waiting for a reasonable grounds decision.

This means those facing homelessness are often left vulnerable to re-exploitation unless they are able to find safe accommodation and support from organisations like ours.

Preventing labour exploitation among people experiencing homelessness

We also act to prevent labour exploitation, using the opportunity to disseminate information and raise guests' awareness of modern slavery. For example, a male guest who had moved out to work on a construction site returned to the hostel because there had been an attempt to take his documents. We had previously informed him about signs

of labour exploitation. On another case, a female guest was offered what sounded like an abusive job as a housekeeper. Our caseworker used this opportunity to provide her with information about labour exploitation in her native language, which led the guest to seek another job, this time with good conditions.

Glass Door also runs an Employability Project, which provides our guests with valuable information about employment rights and identifying exploitative work. In addition, our full-time Employment Advisor, based at partnering drop-in centres, supports people to find safe employment and sustainable routes off the street.

Challenges ahead: risk of exploitation of migrant rough sleepers

Despite our best efforts to support those facing homelessness to exit and steer clear from exploitative jobs, inadequate government policies and the 'hostile environment' rhetoric continue to undermine responses to address modern slavery.

In 2017, a successful legal challenge overturned a Home Office policy that deemed 'rough sleeping' an abuse of rights under the European Union's Free Movement Directive; in practice this policy had resulted in the arrest, detention and removal of vulnerable, homeless Europeans. The High Court judged the policy to be unlawful and discriminatory.

The damage however was done. The policy resulted in the disengagement of street homeless populations with homelessness services and an enduring distrust of the Home Office among homelessness organisations.

Further, it set a precedent. With Brexit and the end of free movement, the criminalisation of the migrant homeless population continues. Last year, the Home Office introduced changes to its immigration rules that stipulate a person's leave can be cancelled or denied if they are found sleeping rough. These multipronged attacks by the Government end up disproportionately discriminating against the most vulnerable and perpetuate a culture of fear against the statutory services that are there to provide protection.

By joining LEAG, Glass Door is giving a platform to the marginalised and disenfranchised populations we work with. Through discussion, information-sharing and collaboration with LEAG members who all work directly with people who have experienced or are at risk of labour exploitation in the UK, we can collaboratively advocate for justice and challenge policies and practices that are putting people at risk of labour exploitation.

27 September 2021

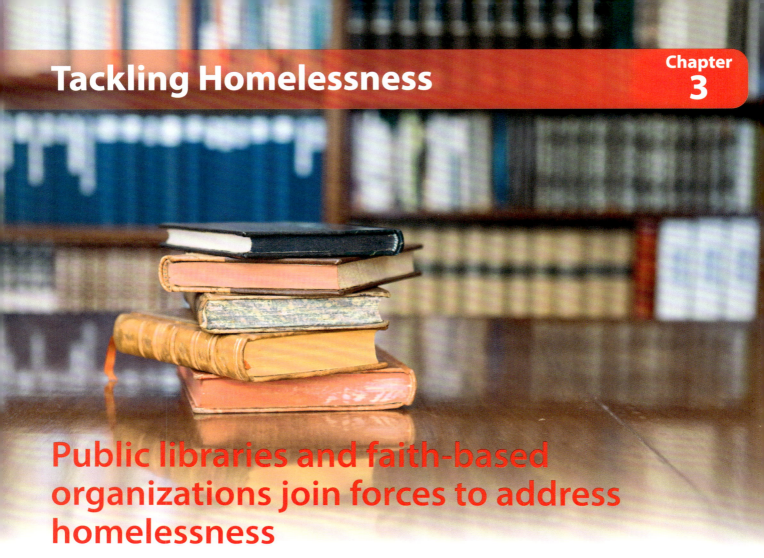

Public libraries and faith-based organizations join forces to address homelessness

An article from *The Conversation*.

THE CONVERSATION

By Kaitlin Wynia Baluk, Postdoctoral fellow in Health and Society, McMaster University

The COVID-19 pandemic has exacerbated homelessness. Throughout the pandemic, shelters reduced capacity to comply with public health protocols, people lost jobs and affordable housing remained elusive.

With a rise in tent cities and makeshift accommodations, homelessness has gained visibility.

Local municipal authorities across Canada have worked to enforce bylaws. Many have dismantled encampments to the dismay of activists and homeless people.

These events, media coverage, ensuing protests and policy discussions raise important questions about public space: How should it be used? Who is the public? And the question I am concerned with here, what are the implications of pushing people who are homeless out of these 'inclusive spaces'?

Homelessness stigma in public spaces

Public spaces, such as parks and sidewalks, are typically thought to belong to everyone. However, many scholars have emphasised that there are rules and unsaid expectations that include and exclude.

Very few spaces exist where people who are homeless can feel like they belong.

Bylaws that criminalise behaviours associated with homelessness – like panhandling – and hostile architecture – like a street bench with a central armrest that prevents people from lying down – are ways of pushing people out of a particular space.

Excluding homeless people from public spaces can perpetuate stigmas. These social stigmas typically take the form of labelling, stereotyping, a separation of 'us and them' and a loss of social status. Sociologist Ervin Goffman famously described stigma as 'a spoiled identity' based on stereotypes rather than inherent qualities.

Homelessness stigmas discredit individuals from participating in social life and limit access to social resources. These stigmas work against efforts to address homelessness because they can lead people to avoid essential services.

Social infrastructure

A natural approach to addressing stigma is to bring people together by forming relationships — in personal relationships, people know each other's personal stories and aspirations, making them less inclined to rely on prejudice and harmful stereotypes.

Brené Brown, who researches courage, vulnerability, shame and empathy captures the essence of this idea with her catchphrase: 'People are hard to hate close up. Move in.' And social infrastructure is the systems and environments that facilitate encounters and relationships, so social scientists have positioned social infrastructure as an antidote to social inequality and fragmentation.

Examples of social infrastructure include community centres, schools and public ice rinks; any space where people can meet and establish social relationships. Social infrastructure is essential to community wellness, it offers grounds for people to pool resources, receive and offer support and navigate social differences.

Strong social infrastructure is accessible, safe and malleable to the public's shifting interests, needs and challenges. Excluding those who are homeless from public spaces not only deepens stigmas that lead to the avoidance of essential services. It can also further marginalise them from the benefits of participating in communal life.

Spaces for people who are homeless

Thankfully, some institutions seek to offer public spaces for people who are homeless. Public libraries and faith-based organizations, such as mosques, churches and non-profits grounded in religious belief, are two examples. While public libraries and faith- based organizations are both quintessential examples of social infrastructure, they differ in significant ways.

Both have strengths and limitations when it comes to creating social connections. Faith-based organizations can be spaces where deep friendships form. These organizations bring people together regularly into a social and spiritual environment. However, they also have several barriers, such as history or reputation of excluding based on identity.

In contrast, a core value of public librarianship is to remove barriers to services.

Public libraries offer free services, regardless of socio-economic, housing and citizenship status, age, gender, ability, religion, sexual orientation, race or culture. Often described as a 'community hub,' public libraries bring people together from all walks of life. Nevertheless, they must balance their enormous mandate to address the informational, learning and leisure needs of diverse populations with bounded resources.

Partnering for stronger social infrastructure

While these two institutions alone may not be able to solve the issue of social stigma, looking at how they provide spaces for homeless people is a good place to start.

Hamilton Public Library's Parkdale branch in Ontario is an example of a partnership between a faith-based organization and a public library. This library branch is in an affordable housing residence, operated by Indwell.

Indwell describes itself as 'a Christian charity that creates affordable housing communities that support people seeking health, wellness and belonging.' As the Parkdale branch only recently opened in July 2021, it presents a budding opportunity to examine how these two types of social infrastructure coalesce to provide inclusive social spaces for people who are homeless.

Partnerships between organizations with shared interests and complementary strengths hold promise when it comes to developing novel solutions to complex problems.

There are several examples of both faith-based organizations and public libraries sharing their spaces with social workers, health-care professionals and local enterprises.

For example, a pilot project in Philadelphia showed that having a social worker and a nurse working in a public library from 9 a.m. to 5 p.m. helped connect homeless people with appropriate health care. The authors attributed some of this intervention's success to the public library's financially accessible community space. Partnerships allow organizations to do more than they could alone for those who are homeless.

Looking for creative ways to strengthen social infrastructure for marginalised groups may be an important step towards building a more equitable society post-COVID-19.

19 October 2021

Roll out Housing First nationally, and we can end rough sleeping once and for all

By Brooks Newmark

Homelessness, and rough sleeping in particular, remains a blight in our society. If the Government is seeking to 'level up' the country then there is no better place to begin than with those at their lowest ebb – rough sleepers.

I have been engaged in the sector for over 30 years, usually as a volunteer, helping out either on the streets at a soup kitchen or at a hostel. I have always believed that there is no reason why a country as wealthy as ours cannot end rough sleeping once and for all. In 2016, with the support of the Centre for Social Justice, Crisis and a Panel of Experts from the sector, which I chaired, I began to work on trying to find a more permanent solution to what looked like the endemic problem of rough sleeping. We looked at best practices in the UK, the US and Europe. In particular, we focused on Finland's 'Housing First' programme, which had all but eradicated rough sleeping.

Housing First does not set preconditions to housing, but recognises that many long-term rough sleepers have what are referred to as 'complex issues' (usually a combination of mental health problems, family breakdown and addiction). What Housing First in essence offers rough sleepers is a permanent home with some form of support to help them address the issues they face.

In 2017 with the support of the CSJ, we produced a report *Housing First: Housing-led Solutions to Rough Sleeping and Homelessness*. The report recommended that the Government consider developing a nationwide Housing First program as a key instrument to eradicate long-term rough sleeping. With evidence from the Joseph Rowntree Foundation we showed that for every £1 spent on providing Housing First support for rough sleepers the Government would save about £2.40 (through emergency healthcare and other areas), in addition, of course, to providing dignity and a better future for rough sleepers.

The then Housing Secretary Sajid Javid read the report, visited Finland, and was so impressed with Housing First that he recommended to the Prime Minister and the Chancellor that we pilot the scheme in Liverpool, Manchester and the West Midlands. The Government invested £28m in those three pilots. After three years, they have already helped over 550 individuals off the streets and into permanent accommodation and, equally importantly, almost nine out of ten individuals have sustained their tenancies, having in the past been unable to do so.

This week the CSJ have produced a follow-up report 'Close to Home: Delivering a National Housing First Programme in England' (homelessness is a devolved matter). Following the evidence from the pilots, the CSJ report recommends to the Government that they roll out a national Housing First Programme. The report has identified about 16,450 people who suffer from a combination of homelessness, mental health issues, drug or alcohol dependency and related behavioural issues, and calls for a three-year investment of approximately £150 million a year to provide Housing First support for the above cohort. The savings estimated are more conservative than in the 2017 report, but still come out at £1.56 savings to the Government for every £1 spent.

The 'Everyone-In' programme, initiated at the start of the pandemic by Housing Secretary Robert Jenrick and then Homelessness Tsar Louise Casey, has housed almost 30,000 individuals. It has also demonstrated that with the right political will we can quickly and effectively address the issue of rough sleeping as well as save lives – which the 'Everyone-In' scheme certainly did.

However, as a recent National Audit Office report has pointed out, there is already evidence that some who benefitted from the 'Everyone-In' programme are already returning to the streets and rough sleeping. Many of these individuals fit the profile for needing Housing First support. As the furlough scheme unwinds and the 'Everyone-In' support scheme ends, there is a risk the trickle of individuals returning to the streets escalates throughout 2021.

The Government has committed to ending rough sleeping by the end of 2024. Working with local government and the voluntary sector, the Government should continue to build on excellent programmes like the Rough Sleepers Initiative and the Housing First pilot schemes in Liverpool, Manchester and the West Midlands by rolling out Housing First nationally.

If the Government wishes to level up society, there is no better place to begin than at the bottom, by providing permanent housing, support and dignity for rough sleepers – Housing First offers them a golden opportunity to do so.

25 February 2021

Brooks Newmark was Minister for Civil Society and currently sits on the Government's Rough Sleepers Advisory Panel.
Columns are the author's own opinion and do not necessarily reflect the views of CapX.

UK's largest purpose-built village for rough sleepers planned in Manchester

Embassy Village will provide 40 purpose-built pods underneath railway arches in desirable Castlefield district.

By Helen Pidd, North of England editor

Plans are under way to build the UK's largest village for rough sleepers in one of Manchester's most desirable neighbourhoods. Embassy Village will provide homes for 40 men in purpose-built pods underneath 10 railway arches in the Castlefield district, where one-bedroom flats regularly sell for £250,000.

Sandwiched between the River Irwell and the Bridgewater canal, the land has been given for free on a 125-year lease by Peel Group, the developers behind MediaCity and the Manchester Ship Canal.

The village is the brainchild of Sid Williams, founder of a Christian charity called Embassy. A skinny-jeaned, perma-cheerful enthusiast, he ran a homeless shelter on Mumford & Sons' old tour bus until Covid got in the way.

James Whittaker, Peel's executive director of development, calls him Jesus, 'because you can't help but feel the genuine good he's doing. He's probably the kindest, most genuine man I've ever met.'

Though he would blush at the blasphemous comparison, 36-year-old Williams has a remarkable knack for getting rich people to dig into their pockets in his mission to house the homeless and destitute in Manchester.

An estate agent would describe Embassy Village as 'waterside living in a city centre location'. Showing the Guardian around the site last month, Williams admitted it currently looks more like 'an apocalyptic wasteland', with water dripping from two viaducts carrying noisy trams and trains and some rough sleepers having already set up mattresses among the detritus of illegal raves.

Planning permission was granted this summer, with 61% of local people in favour of the project. Now Williams – helped by Tim Heatley, founder of property developer Capital & Centric and chair of the Greater Manchester mayor's homelessness charity – is on a mission to raise £3m to build the village, offering local corporates a chance to sponsor one or more homes.

Computer-generated simulations of the project show alfresco dining, festoon lighting and imaginary residents tending to communal gardens – exactly the sort of aspirational images sold to wealthy young professionals moving into the skyscrapers popping up across Manchester. But while they may pay £800 a month for a one-bed studio, Embassy's residents are likely to pay no more than the local housing allowance – currently £302 a month for a room in a shared house or £552 for a one-bed flat.

Embassy is not providing 'forever' homes. Residents can stay for a maximum of two years. The idea is to 'give every resident a live trial run at managing a home, cooking, cleaning and paying rent in a sympathetic and supported environment', said Williams.

The site of Embassy Village lies on derelict land beneath 10 railway arches which lie adjacent to the Mancunian Way and Bridgewater Canal, opposite modern canalside apartments.

Running the Embassy bus led Williams to conclude that shelters are not really the answer to solving rough sleeping. If people are to get off the streets, they need stable tenancies and wrap-around support. They also need jobs, which is why Embassy partners with 18 local businesses who agree to give interviews and hopefully employment to its tenants.

To qualify for residency in Embassy Village, residents must be men with no alcohol or drug addictions. (Embassy will soon open a separate, more low-key project for homeless women fleeing domestic violence.) As well as paying rent, they must commit to six hours a week of training in shopping, cooking and budgeting. 'I wanted to get away from the shelter model where you sort of accidentally become a parent, going, 'Oh, I'll do the shopping. And I'll do the cleaning. And I'll do the cooking,'' said Williams.

The preconception that most homeless people are addicts is not true, said Williams: 'Sixty per cent of our chaps are homeless because of relationship breakdowns.'

During the pandemic, Embassy rented properties to move men from the tour bus into homes, including one who had spent seven years in shelters waiting for a council house. With about 13,000 households on the waiting list in Manchester, he never got to the top as a 'single bloke with no criminal record, no addictions and no real mental health struggles', said Williams.

Potential residents will be referred by Manchester city council or local homeless charities and then interviewed by Embassy. 'The interview is really to ascertain whether you're serious about change,' said Williams. 'Believe it or not, about half the people we interview say, 'I don't want a job, I don't ever want to work, I want to live in a council flat. That's my ambition.' And we go, 'That's great. But we are not that thing.''

Smaller homeless villages have been built in recent years in Bristol and Edinburgh, and the Hope Gardens development in Ealing, west London, has 60 apartments in containers used as emergency accommodation in 20ft containers for the newly homeless.

What makes Embassy different is the ambition to build a community. Central to this is a village hall, complete with counselling room, laundry and communal computers, plus a training kitchen to help residents learn to cook, said Williams: 'That way we can be a community, we watch England lose at the football, we can celebrate people's birthdays, and Christmas dinner – all that good stuff.'

1 November 2021

Long-term funding essential to supporting veterans experiencing homelessness

By Lee Buss-Blair

Riverside, Stoll, Alabaré and Launchpad are the four main providers of supported housing for veterans in the United Kingdom. Director of Operations at Riverside Lee Buss-Blair tells us how they have been working together to highlight the growing crisis they face and the significant risk of collapse of specialist housing for homeless veterans.

Understanding the full extent of veteran homelessness is difficult, as there is a lack of consistency across local government and the third sector when it comes to capturing data relating to someone's status as a veteran.

Latest estimates indicate that between 100 and 400 veterans sleep rough ever year and a further 3,000 to 4,000 face homelessness in cars, or derelict buildings – something no veteran or civilian should experience. The most recent CHAIN Data indicates 5% of rough sleepers were veterans, and this data has ranged between 3% and 4% for many years. Veterans make up 5% of the UK population, so veterans are not overrepresented in the rough sleeper population.

You often see on social media wild claims that veterans make up 10%, sometimes 25%, of the rough sleeping population. This simply isn't true, and these claims primarily come from groups with an agenda to argue for not helping other groups, migrants for example, and not to get support for veterans.

But veteran homelessness is still an issue, and veteran specific supported housing plays a key role.

What makes veterans homelessness different?

I've worked in Homelessness for over 20 years, and I know that good quality mainstream supported housing can effectively meet the needs of veterans. One of the key issues mainstream and veteran supported housing is the impact of trauma, and the models we, as a sector, use to work with trauma are effective irrespective of the cause.

However, as a combat veteran with PTSD, I also know that we are really bad at seeking help. We are taught in the military that we are different to civilians, dare I say it, better, and that civilians couldn't do what we do. This is an important part of building a strong bond, critical for ensuring that a unit can function in high stress situations. But nobody has really considered the long term impact of this. I avoided accessing mainstream mental health services for a good 10 years, using the 'they wouldn't understand' excuse.

It has already been recognised that, in some circumstances, special treatment may be appropriate to overcome barriers to engagement. Armed forces veterans suffering a mental health crisis now receive specialist care as part of a new Op COURAGE service launched by NHS. NHS staff will work with military charities to provide therapy, rehab services and, in extreme cases, inpatient care to hundreds of former soldiers, sailors and RAF personnel each year. Involving charities will help NHS staff to understand the experiences and issues faced by those who have risked their lives for their country and may have lost comrades or been injured themselves.

We are asking for the same recognition to be given to veteran supported housing. Over the past few years, veteran supported housing services have lost nearly all government funding. As a result of this we are becoming significantly less able to house veterans with higher needs, addictions, poor mental health, or disability.

If this continues, we are very concerned about our ability to resource veterans' services safely, and the significant risk of collapse of the majority of supported housing services for veterans.

Too many veterans, when given the choice of engaging in mainstream services or not engaging, are likely to choose not to engage at all.

Our concern is that, in the absence of properly funded veteran supported housing, veterans with significant support needs experiencing homelessness will avoid accessing mainstream homelessness services, and end up on the streets as a result.

The threat identified to veteran supported housing is real, and we have raised it now with a clear and achievable response in mind. It would cost just £2,781,985 per year to provide specialist supported housing to every veteran in the UK which needs it.

We are asking Government for funding for at least two years until the end of this parliament, which is £5,563,970, with a view of agreeing the mechanism for long-term sustainable funding to ensure these much-needed services continue.

So to ensure that this critical issue is put firmly on the Government's agenda we are asking the sector to get behind our campaign for this funding – to include this call for much needed veterans' funding in any conversations you are having and to get behind and share our social media campaign.

15 October 2021

Lee Buss-Blair is Director of Operations at Riverside.

'They will change lives': the micro houses tackling homelessness in Cambridge

In the shadows of its famous university, people are living rough in Cambridge. A new housing project aims to address that.

By Gavin Haines

An affordable housing project delayed by coronavirus will launch next week, providing secure accommodation to rough sleepers in Cambridge, where the high cost of living has pushed people onto the street.

The development comprises six micro homes, which have been installed on land belonging to a local church. The land has been donated to the project for three years and the properties have been designed to be easily relocated to another free site when the current tenure is up.

Each property has a fitted kitchen, living area, bathroom, separate bedroom and washing machine. Residents can stay for as long as they need and will receive onsite support from the homeless charity Jimmy's Cambridge.

When the units are moved to another location, residents will have the choice of continuing to live in them or moving to more permanent accommodation if they are able to do so.

The initiative has been led by the charity Allia, which supports development projects with a positive impact, in partnership with Jimmy's and the New Meaning Foundation, an ethical construction social enterprise.

'One of the main challenges facing people who are homeless is finding affordable accommodation together with the support to help deal with the causes of what led them to sleeping rough on the streets in the first place,' said Mark Allan, chief executive of Jimmy's Cambridge.

'This project offers both. Six new affordable homes backed up with a team of committed, caring staff and volunteers with expertise in supporting people deal with their addictions, build their self-worth and tackle their mental health difficulties, reconnect with estranged family, find employment, and so much more. These new homes will change people's lives.'

A 2018 report by Centre for Cities, a think tank, declared Cambridge the most unequal city in the UK. In the shadow of its famous university many people are living rough due partly to a lack of affordable housing.

'We hope this will be the start of more such innovative projects until there is enough housing for all who need it,' said Martin Clark, group director of impact at Allia. 'We're excited to finally launch these homes and hope they will make a real difference to people's lives.'

The homes were funded by grants and donations from public and private sector companies and were built by workers at the New Meaning Foundation, which provides employment for people with experience of homelessness.

'Building the units offered a great opportunity for training and work experience to 13 young people from a homeless background, building their skills, confidence and self-belief in the process,' said John Evans, director of the New Meaning Foundation.

15 June 2020

What should you do if you see a homeless person?

A warm greeting and a word or two can make all the difference this Christmas.

By Liam Geraghty

Homelessness has become a clearly visible issue on Britain's streets in recent years and as temperatures drop over Christmas it can be a perilous time to be on the street.

So that means it is also the time when you can make the most difference.

There may be less people on the street generally this Christmas due to the impact of Covid-19 but for many people experiencing homelessness who are not able to access support, the streets will still be a place to stay.

Official figures showed 2,688 people were estimated to be sleeping rough on a single night in autumn 2020, according to England's official count.

And the figure is also 52 per cent higher than in 2010 when the current counting system began and the Conservatives came into power.

The stats put in perspective the challenge that the current Westminster government is facing to reach its target of ending rough sleeping by 2024.

Devolved countries Scotland and Wales are also working to eradicate rough sleeping – the most visible form of homelessness.

But the sight of someone living on the streets remains commonplace but there are a number of ways where you can have a big impact on someone's life for a small investment in time, particularly during the festive season.

What do you say to a homeless person?

The first way to help homeless people is a simple one – speak up! A warm greeting, some simple small talk or even just asking a personal question can make all the difference.

Homelessness puts an enormous strain on mental health with long hours of loneliness, isolation and sleep deprivation.

And while Christmas can be a joyous celebration for most people, for others it can be a difficult time, especially if, like many people experiencing homelessness, they are excluded from festivities or spend the time alone.

Big Issue vendors can have this experience, too, even while out selling the magazine on a packed street.

That's why speaking up is so important.

Just think that the person that you pass who is living on the streets might not have spoken to anyone that day – just a simple 'hello, how are you?' could make an enormous difference to someone's day.

And who knows? Maybe you will take away something that does the same for you.

So why not strike up a conversation? And if you get chatting to one of our *Big Issue* vendors working hard to earn a living on the streets this Christmas, why not buy a magazine too?

What would you ask a homeless person?

Striking up a conversation is no different than with anyone else. You can say hello, ask how someone is or what plans they have for Christmas.

The same rules apply to striking up a conversation with any stranger, just be friendly and respectful and be wary of overstepping any boundaries. Many people will strike up a conversation, others might not want to talk. That's fine, too, it's all about making sure the other person is comfortable.

As well as asking how they are doing, you could also see if they need any help with anything.

Homelessness also makes it almost impossible for rough sleepers to access services that those with a secure home can often take for granted. Healthcare can be tricky to get while setting up essential facilities required for work or benefits, like a bank account, are also tough without an address.

StreetLink becomes increasingly crucial for finding people who are homeless but may be out of sight on the streets – when the temperature drops accessing emergency support can quickly become life-saving.

As the weather turns colder this winter, living on the streets becomes ever more dangerous. Heatwaves can become just as deadly too while climate change means extreme weather events are likely to become more frequent.

Official statistics showed 688 people died in England without a secure home in 2020 while 216 people died in Scotland. While interventions you can make on the street may seem like a small thing, they can also potentially save someone's life.

If you have an immediate concern for someone who is unwell or in danger on the street, call the emergency services.

What is the best thing to give a homeless person?

Life on the streets is tough and some of the challenges change from season to season.

In the winter, give a warm drink, warm clothing and other things that insulate from the cold if you are unable to help get the person to shelter.

Summer can be just as difficult with no place to get out of the sun. So consider offering high-factor sunscreen – which can often be expensive – and water to rough sleepers to protect them from the heat.

And if you see any of our vendors out selling the magazine on a pitch near you, a warm word would not go amiss alongside supporting them by buying the magazine.

Of course, you could always put a homeless person in touch with one of our distribution offices all over the UK to give them the chance to get themselves a hand up, not a hand out too.

But it is important to have a compassionate and non-judgmental conversation with the person you are trying to help first. They can tell you what they want and what help they might need. They may not want anything at all, it is up to them.

9 December 2021

£316 million government funding boost to tackle homelessness

The Homelessness Prevention Grant will support households in England who are homeless or at risk of losing their home.

From: Department for Levelling Up, Housing and Communities and Eddie Hughes MP

- **Homelessness Prevention Grant will support the homeless and those at risk of losing their home**
- **Councils will use the funding to help people find a new home, get help with evictions, or move into temporary accommodation**
- **Funding includes £5.8 million for those forced into homelessness by domestic abuse**

Tens of thousands of people will be protected from homelessness as a result of a £316 million funding boost, announced by the Department for Levelling Up, Housing and Communities today (21 December 2021).

The government's Homelessness Prevention Grant will support households in England who are homeless or at risk of losing their home. Councils will use the funding to help them find a new home, access support for unexpected evictions and secure temporary accommodation where needed.

The funding includes an additional £5.8 million to support people forced into homelessness by domestic abuse. This follows the landmark Domestic Abuse Act, which ensures councils give people who find themselves in this situation a 'priority need' for assistance.

Funding will be allocated to all councils responsible for housing in England based on local homelessness need in individual areas.

This underlines the government's commitment to ensure people at risk of becoming homeless, across the country, get help more quickly. Since the Homelessness Reduction Act came into force in 2018, over 400,000 households

have been successfully prevented from losing their homes or supported into settled accommodation, with rough sleeping levels falling 37% between 2019 and 2020.

Minister for Rough Sleeping Eddie Hughes MP said:

'I have seen first-hand the devastation of those who come face to face with homelessness, and my heart goes out to anyone in this situation.

The support we are announcing today is going directly to communities that need it most.

It will help thousands of people across England, with councils able to prevent homelessness before it occurs and put a roof over the heads of those who have lost their homes'

Cllr James Jamieson, Local Government Association Chairman, said:

'It is really important that we focus on avoiding the tragedy of people becoming homeless in the first place.

This vital funding will help councils support households to remain in their homes for as long as possible, and find alternative safe, secure housing for those that need it.

We are also pleased government is providing additional funding so councils can further support those made homeless as a result of suffering domestic abuse.'

Jon Sparkes, Chief Executive of Crisis, said:

'To end homelessness we need to prevent people being forced from their homes in the first place, so this funding for vital local authority services is very welcome.

With the appalling rise in domestic abuse during lockdowns and the pandemic forcing many more into homelessness, it is especially important that councils in England will have more money to provide accommodation for survivors.'

Lord Bird, Founder of The Big Issue, said:

'I am delighted to see the government investing in homelessness prevention and support for people at risk of losing their homes or being evicted.

The worrying number of people in rent arrears and at risk of eviction because of the pandemic has kept me up at night for months. Hearing that the government are taking action to stop mass homelessness from becoming a reality is a great relief.

This will save an avalanche of people from the damaging experience of homelessness – as well as saving the Treasury millions on all the associated costs. This is exactly the kind of step in the right direction that we need, shifting the focus to prevention and long-term thinking rather than waiting for the crisis happens.'

The Homelessness Prevention Grant, available for 2022/23, is on top of the recently-announced £66 million to provide rough sleepers with safe and warm accommodation and drug and alcohol treatment services this winter, and £65 million support package for vulnerable renters struggling due to the impact of the pandemic. Overall, the government is investing £2 billion over the next three years to tackle homelessness and rough sleeping.

Government has also announced a £28 million funding boost to help rough sleepers get their COVID-19 vaccines and move into safe accommodation. The Protect and Vaccinate scheme will help to increase vaccine uptake among people who are homeless and sleeping rough, by supporting outreach work in shelters to educate people about the dangers of the virus, giving money to councils to provide safe and secure accommodation while their level of vaccination is increased and delivering mobile vaccinations.

Recent funding has enabled local councils across the country to deliver practical, on the ground support for homeless people.

Calderdale Council in West Yorkshire, for example, has used government funding to provide 25 units of self-contained flats and long term accommodation to help prevent homelessness and drive down the number of rough sleepers in the local area. These units offer a range of on-site support for residents including support on how best to 'Move on' and an NHS run Wound Clinic to treat emergency injuries and provide access to sexual health, drug and alcohol services.

Cllr Scott Patient, Calderdale Council's Cabinet Member for Climate Change and Resilience, said:

'We understand the impact that rough sleeping and homelessness can have on individuals, families and communities. Everyone affected has their own story, and the circumstances can be very complex and distressing. We do all we can, working with local partner organisations, to offer people hope and a stronger future through support, advice and accommodation.

We have made significant progress, and every step we've taken has brought hope to those living street-based lifestyles, helping them to rebuild their lives. We know there is still more to do, and the financial support from the government helps us to make this happen.

One Calderdale service user is John, 49, who now has a long-term tenancy after a member of the public found him rough sleeping in a tent in the undergrowth in Sowerby Bridge, Calderdale.'

John was assessed for a Rough Sleeping Accommodation Programme-funded, long-term tenancy, but was nervous to take this on as he had never had his own home. He was offered reassurance around the support he would have to help him to sustain the tenancy. He wanted to remain close to his mum and a suitable property was identified to facilitate this. John was supported to open his first bank account, change the location of his prescription, contact utility suppliers and register with a new doctor.

Whilst having a tenancy was a huge leap for John, this was made easier with assistance from his support worker. Having his own property has given him a new lease of life and stability, and the platform where he can address his substance misuse. He has a blossoming relationship and he is able to live an independent life in the comfort of knowing that he has staff and support services around him should he need it.

John said:

'From getting out of the tent in Sowerby Bridge and meeting the support services, I don't think I'd be here today. I feel alive, better, stronger in myself, more confident, no drugs. Without support I wouldn't be here.'

21 December 2021

Key Facts

- Homelessness charity Crisis estimates that up to 62% of homeless people do not show up on official figures. (page 1)

- The Homelessness Reduction Act, passed in 2017, provided a legal duty that should enable all homeless people to receive help from their local council. This homelessness legislation specified that councils must try to prevent people becoming homeless in the first place. Councils started delivering their new duties on 3 April 2018. (page 1)

- At the peak of the COVID-19 pandemic, the government's 'Everyone in Scheme' protected more than 37,000 rough sleepers. (page 2)

- The Charity Shelter suggested that 280,000 people were homeless in England as of December 2019. (page 2)

- People sleeping on the street are almost 17 times more likely to have been victims of violence and 15 times more likely to have suffered verbal abuse compared to the general public. (page 2)

- More than 30,000 households applied for homelessness assistance in Wales between April 2019 and March 2020. (page 3)

- Official rough sleeping statistics showed the number of people living on the streets fell in England during the Covid-19 pandemic with an estimated 2,688 people sleeping rough on a single night in autumn 2020. This was a 37 per cent decrease on the 4,266 people recorded in 2019 and was the third straight year in which the count showed a decrease. (page 6)

- However, the 2020 figure was still 52 per cent higher than the 1,247 people counted as sleeping rough in 2010. Rough sleeping has increased steadily over the last decade. (page 6)

- In 2018/19, nearly £1 billion less was spent on support services for single homeless people than was spent in 2008/09 (Homeless Link) (page 6)

- 52% of the British public believe homelessness is a consequence of societal issues outside a person's control rather than down to a person's poor choices. (page 7)

- MOH's (Museum of Homelessness) latest count revealed 976 homeless people died across England, Wales, Scotland and Northern Ireland in 2020 – a rise of 37 per cent on the previous 2019 tally. (page 7)

- Nearly half (44%) of all people recorded as sleeping rough on a single night in autumn 2020 were in London and the South East. (page 13)

- 85% of all people recorded as sleeping rough on a single night in autumn 2020 were male. (page 13)

- 87% of all people recorded as sleeping rough on a single night in autumn 2020 were aged 26 and over. (page 13)

- 72% of all people recorded as sleeping rough on a single night in autumn 2020 were UK nationals. (page 13)

- According to governement statistics, 8,319 young people registered as homeless in Scotland in 2019/20220. (page 15)

- Homelessness charity Streetlink recorded 16,976 alets made by the public about rough sleepers between April and June 2020 (page 17)

- People experiencing mental health problems are more susceptible to becoming homeless, and the stresses of becoming homeless are more likely to amplify poor mental health. This was represented by a 2014 study, which found that 80% of homeless people in England reported that they had mental health issues and 45% that they had been diagnosed with a mental health condition. (page 22)

- Insecure housing is a key issue for survivors of modern slavery, as highlighted in a recently published report by Crisis. The research documented the experience of over 330 people from across the UK affected by homelessness and modern slavery over the past two years. Labour exploitation was identified as the second most common type of exploitation after sexual exploitation overall; however, it was the most prevalent type of exploitation among men facing homelessness. (page 28)

- The Government has committed to ending rough sleeping by the end of 2024. (page 32)

- Latest estimates indicate that between 100 and 400 veterans sleep rough ever year and a further 3,000 to 4,000 face homelessness in cars, or derelict buildings. (page 34)

- 216 people died in Scotland without a secure home in 2020. (page 37)

- Since the Homelessness Reduction Act came into force in 2018, over 400,000 households have been successfully prevented from losing their homes or supported into settled accommodation, with rough sleeping levels falling 37% between 2019 and 2020. (page 38)

Emergency accommodation

Short-term housing for those in urgent need.

Eviction

An eviction is a legal process through which a landlord can make a tenant vacate a property.

Hidden homelessness

In addition to those people recognised as statutory homeless, there are also a large number of homeless single adults, or couples without dependent children, who meet the legal definition of homelessness but not the criteria for priority need. In many cases they will not even apply for official recognition, knowing they do not meet the criteria. Statistics provided by the Government will therefore not include all people in the country who actually meet the definition of homeless. As a result, this group is often referred to as the hidden homeless.

Homelessness

The law defines somebody as being homeless if they do not have a legal right to occupy any accommodation or if their accommodation is unsuitable to live in. This can cover a wide range of circumstances, including, but not restricted to, the following: having no accommodation at all; having accommodation that is not reasonable to live in, even in the short-term (e.g because of violence or health reasons); having a legal right to accommodation that for some reason you cannot access (e.g you have been illegally evicted); living in accommodation you have no legal right to occupy (e.g living in a squat or temporarily staying with friends).

Homelessness and mental health

Mental health and housing are closely interlinked: mental ill health can make it difficult for people to maintain good quality housing and can lead to homelessness, whereas homelessness, poor quality housing and housing insecurity can lead to mental health issues. Mental ill health is common among people who experience homelessness and rough sleepers – estimates range from one-third up to 76%. An estimated 43% of clients in an average homelessness project in England are likely to have mental health needs.

Night shelter

Night shelters are a type of basic, temporary accommodation for people who would otherwise be sleeping on the streets.

Priority need

Under homelessness legislation, certain categories of household are considered to have priority need for accommodation. Priority need applies to all households that contain a pregnant woman or are responsible for dependent children; to some households made up of a 16- to 17-year-old or a care leaver aged 18 to 21; or where someone is vulnerable, e.g because of old age, health problems, or by having been in prison, care or the Forces.

Rough sleeping

Rough sleeping is the most visible form of homelessness. Rough sleepers typically sleep outside in the open air on the streets or in parks of a town or city.

Sofa surfing

Sofa surfing is when a person finds themselves without accommodation and relies on family or friends to put them up temporarily, usually on their sofa or floor while they seek more permanent accommodation.

Squatting

If a person is said to be squatting, it means they are occupying a property without the right to do so (e,g they don't pay rent or own the property). Trespassing and squatting in residential buildings (like a house or flat) is illegal and is considered a crime.

Activities

Brainstorming

♦ The term 'homelessness' applies to a wide range of situations in which people can find themselves. In small groups, discuss what you know about homelessness and what you understand by the following terms:

- sofa-surfing

- rough sleeping

- night shelter

- emergency accommodation

- eviction

♦ What is the difference between the 'sheltered homeless' and the 'unsheltered homeless'?

Research

♦ Using the articles in this book, and the internet, do some research into homelessness in the UK and consider the following:

- the causes of homelessness

- the age group most affected by homelessness

- the gender most affected by homelessness

- the ethnic group most affected by homelessness

- the areas in the UK with the highest homelessness statistics

Write a short report and share it with the rest of the class.

♦ Conduct some research online to find out what support services, if any, are available for homeless people in your area, such as night shelters, soup kitchens and charities. Are there any helpful organisations or advisory services for people who find themselves at risk of homelessness?

♦ Select a country other than your own and do some online research about homelessness in that country. Make notes on your findings and how they compare with the homelessness situation in your own country. Feedback to the rest of the class.

♦ In pairs, find out the latest statistics reflecting the number of children in the UK currently living in temporary accommodation. What factors do you think have caused this? What is being done to help their situation? Write up a short report of your findings.

Design

♦ In pairs, draw a homeless person and include short notes describing the following:

- why they became homeless

- where they are sleeping

- what help they are getting

- what you would do to help them.

Share your ideas with the rest of the class.

♦ Imagine you work for a homeless charity. Design a poster to highlight the plight of homeless people. Where do you think would be the best places to display your poster?

♦ Design a 'care package' for a homeless person. What essential items will you include the package and why?

♦ Choose one the articles from this book and create an illustration to accompany it.

Oral

♦ As a class, discuss the following statement:

'People only have themselves to blame if they experience homelessness.'

Is this something the majority of the class agrees with or not?

♦ In small groups think about and discuss what it might mean to have nowhere to live. In what ways would it make life more difficult? What would you miss most about your own home if you suddenly found yourself without it? Compile a list and share with the class.

♦ Read the articles on pages 14 and 15. As a class, discuss the main reasons why a young person could become homeless.

Reading/writing

♦ Imagine you are homeless in one the following situations and write a letter to your MP describing your circumstances and asking for help:

- a parent of three young children sharing one room in temporary B&B accommodation

- a teenager who has been told to leave their home and has no other family to turn to

- a war veteran with PTSD

- a person who can no longer work due to ill health and whose welfare benefits are not enough to cover rent.

♦ Choose one of the articles in this book and write a one paragraph summary. List three of the key points made.

♦ Write a definition of the term 'hidden homeless'.

Acknowledgements

The publisher is grateful for permission to reproduce the material in this book. While every care has been taken to trace and acknowledge copyright, the publisher tenders its apology for any accidental infringement or where copyright has proved untraceable. The publisher would be pleased to come to a suitable arrangement in any such case with the rightful owner.

The material reproduced in **issues** books is provided as an educational resource only. The views, opinions and information contained within reprinted material in **issues** books do not necessarily represent those of Independence Educational Publishers and its employees.

Images

Cover image courtesy of iStock. All other images courtesy Freepik, Pixabay & Unsplash.

Illustrations

Simon Kneebone: pages 4, 25 &37. Angelo Madrid: pages 3, 9 & 34.

Additional acknowledgements

With thanks to the Independence team: Shelley Baldry, and Jackie Staines. Contributing Editor: Tracy Biram

Danielle Lobban

Cambridge, January 2022